Executive Skills
for
Busy School Leaders

by
Christopher Hitch
and
Dave Coley

EYE ON EDUCATION

EYE ON EDUCATION
6 DEPOT WAYWEST, SUITE 106
LARCHMONT, NY 10538
(914) 833–0551
(914) 833–0761 fax
www.eyeoneducation.com

A sincere effort has been made to supply the identity of those who have created specific strategies. Any omissions have been unintentional.

Library of Congress Cataloging-in-Publication Data

Hitch, Christopher.
 Executive skills for busy school leaders / by Christopher Hitch and
Dave Coley.
     p. cm.
 Includes bibliographical references.
 ISBN 978-1-59667-134-8
1. School management and organization. 2. Educational leadership. 3.
Executive ability. 4. School management teams. I. Coley, Dave. II. Title.
 LB2805.H565 2009
 371.2--dc22

                                                        2009030594

10 9 8 7 6 5 4 3 2 1

Production services provided by
Rick Soldin a Book/Print Production Specialist
Jonesborough, TN — www.book-comp.com

Also Available from Eye On Education

Leading School Change: 9 Strategies to Bring Everybody on Board
Todd Whitaker

Get Organized! Time Management for School Leaders
Frank Buck

Classroom Walkthroughs to Improve Teaching and Learning
Donald E. Kachur, Judith A. Stout, and Claudia L. Edwards

The Principalship from A to Z
Ron Williamson and Barbara R. Blackburn

The Principal as Instructional Leader, Second Edition
Sally J. Zepeda

The Instructional Leader's Guide to Informal Classroom Observations, Second Edition
Sally J. Zepeda

Professional Learning Communities: An Implementation Guide and Toolkit
Kathleen A. Foord and Jean M. Haar

Professional Development: What Works
Sally J. Zepeda

Motivating & Inspiring Teachers, Second Edition
Todd Whitaker, Beth Whitaker and Dale Lumpa

Data, Data Everywhere:
Bringing All the Data Together for continuous School Improvement
Victoria L. Bernhardt

Creating School Cultures that Embrace Learning: What Successful Leaders Do
Tony Thacker, John S. Bell and Franklin P. Schargel

From At-Risk to Academic Excellence: What Successful Leaders Do
Franklin P. Schargel, Tony Thacker and John S. Bell

Improving Your Daily Practice: A Guide for Effective School Leadership
Timothy B. Berkey

Help Teachers Engage Students: Action Tools for Administrators
Annette Brinkman, Gary Forlini, and Ellen Williams

For April, David, and Sarah . . . with love and devotion.
Chris

Thanks to my wife, Kenna, for her love and support.
Dave

Meet the Authors

Christopher Hitch has led leadership programs for principals, assistant principals, and assistant superintendents as Assistant Director of the University of North Carolina's Principals' Executive Program (PEP) and Director of the Principal Fellows Program. He has also served as a teacher, the principal of three schools, and a district Human Resources Director and Accountability Director.

One of the four national award winners from the Association of American School Administrators, he now serves as Program Director for Government Executive Development at UNC-Chapel Hill.

In addition to speaking at state and national conferences, Chris frequently leads workshops for school executives and teacher leaders. His most popular topics include Finding Time for Instructional Leadership, Leading Higher Performance, Making Change Stick, Getting the Best From Your Team, and How to Ensure Your School Improvement Efforts Pay Off.

Dave Coley has 30 years experience in public education as a teacher, assistant principal, and principal. When he was principal of Cary High School in North Carolina, his school received the US Department of Education Blue Ribbon award. Dave left Cary High School in 2005 to join the staff of the Principals Executive Program in Chapel Hill, North Carolina.

Currently, Dave teaches in the Master of School Administration program at Western Carolina University and supervises administrative interns across the state. Prior to joining the faculty at Western Carolina, he was the Director of the Leadership Institute for High School Redesign with the North Carolina New Schools Project, funded by the Bill and Melinda Gates Foundation.

Dave is a frequent presenter at regional and national conferences and workshop facilitator for school districts around the country. He also served on the Principal Advisory Board for the National Board for Professional Teaching Standards.

Acknowledgements

We're grateful to Bob Sickles and his patience as we wrote this book while we were doing our day jobs. His encouragement and cajoling helped us to get this book in a format that is useful and workable. Thanks also to all of the professors and experts at the University of North Carolina-Chapel Hill's School of Government, School of Public Health, and the Kenan-Flagler Business School. It's always a pleasure to get a chance to work with and learn from true professionals.

We owe a special debt of gratitude to Brad Sneeden, the former director of the Principals' Executive Program. Brad was an incredible leader, finding ways for us to be successful, helping us when we went down a wrong path, and supporting us in our efforts. Tragically, Brad died suddenly while we were working on the early stages of this book. We hope he's looking down on us and giving us two big thumbs-up.

We wouldn't be able to have written this book without the incredible people of the North Carolina Principals' Executive Program. We had the chance to work with Ken Jenkins, a former director of the Principals' Executive Program, as well as Brad, along with some incredible program directors and faculty. Thanks to all of you who helped us better understand how to translate knowledge into results.

One of our college professors, Julio George, had a profound impact on us, mostly reminding us to focus on substance, not form. Julio, we hope we succeeded by your standards.

We also thank the hundreds of principals, assistant principals, and central office executives who have been kind enough to allow us to work and learn together on what works and what doesn't work in the practical aspects of school leadership. We're richer for it and we hope that we've faithfully outlined the lessons you've shared.

Undoubtedly, we would not have been able to bring this book to you without the support of our families. You've made our corners of the world a bit brighter simply by being a big part of it. Thanks for indulging us, putting up with our weird hours, habits, papers strewn all over the place, and gently asking at just the right moment, "Aren't you finished with that yet?"

Chris Hitch
Dave Coley

Contents

Free Downloads

The tools discussed and displayed in this book are also available on Eye On Education's website as Adobe Acrobat PDF files. Those who have purchased this book have permission to download them and print them out. You can access these downloads by visiting Eye On Education's website: **www.eyeoneducation.com**

Click on FREE Downloads or search or browse our Web site to find this book and then scroll down for downloading instructions.

You'll need your book-buyer access code: **EXE-7134-8**

List of Free Downloads

Introduction

Why You Might Need This Book

You got to where you are because you were an outstanding teacher. You had strong classroom management skills, you were able to bring lessons to life in the classroom, and you were able to differentiate instruction. You received at least 4 years of formal education to prepare you for your first teaching job. Yet, in many cases, that first year in the classroom was a trial by fire. It wasn't that your formal education didn't prepare you. It was simply that the demands and nuances of the job, every eventuality, could not be anticipated.

As you gained more experience, people started looking to you for leadership. Your principal set you up to take on more leadership roles, possibly as a grade level or department chair. You probably went back to school to get graduate education in school administration or leadership. You were promoted to your first assistant principalship, and then principalship. Each new situation required new knowledge and skills.

We've written this book to take advantage of the wisdom and experience that we've gained from our work as school leaders as well as the wisdom of school principals that we've been proud to work with and learn from. We've also brought in wisdom from outside the traditional education field. We've brought in perspectives from senior leaders in federal government, the military, and the business world. We've found that these perspectives provide a richer background and insight that can help you become even more effective in your daily work.

As Admiral Gary Roughead, the Chief of Naval Operations (akin to the CEO of the United States Navy) noted in his March 2008 comments to all Navy admirals , "It's about . . . not trying to turn the Navy into a business, but to understand the business of the Navy. . . ." If you are an assistant principal, you'll find practical tools to help you make the shift from being a teacher to being a school leader. If you are a new principal, you'll find numerous models and ideas that can help you thrive in your first principalship, rather than simply surviving it. We don't believe that you can avoid all of the inevitable potholes of your first principalship. This book, however, can help you avoid some typical issues that a novice principal encounters. If you are an experienced principal, you'll find some strategies and perspectives that can help you become even more effective in helping all students succeed.

How This Book Came to You

This book was created through a series of serendipitous events. The authors were reacquainted while waiting in a long line to vote during an election. During the inevitable "20 questions," we found that both of us had been working with school leaders in various capacities. Dave had spent time as a middle school principal and high school principal. He won local and national awards for his schools' success and opened up a new middle school, starting it from scratch. He was also teaching at the university level.

Chris had spent time as an elementary school principal, math consultant, and HR/accountability director at the central office level. He had also spent time in the private sector, running a multinational line of business. At the time we reacquainted, Chris was leading professional development activities at the North Carolina Principals' Executive Program. When an opening became available, Dave applied and received the job offer at the Principals' Executive Program.

We then worked together to design and deliver professional development for aspiring principals, new principals, and experienced principals. We found we had complementary skills and backgrounds that resulted in high impact workshops and seminars around the state. During our seminars, we thought about collaborating on a book together. We went separate ways, Dave to the North Carolina New Schools Project and Chris to the work in executive development with navy admirals, army generals, and other senior leaders in the federal government. We kept in touch, conducted workshops together, and presented at national conferences. Bob Sickles, the CEO of Eye on Education, came up to us after one of these and offered his help to transform the insights from a workshop format to writing a book so that we could help a larger number of school executives. Through late nights and early mornings with coffee, we worked to bring the research and practical application from a workshop setting to this book. We hope you find it helpful and practical in your professional development.

1
Moving into a New Role

At some point in your career, you may start thinking about your next challenge. You may have been confirmed for a new role within your school district, or you may be a finalist for a new position. The decisions you make during your first 90 days on the job can set the course for your entire tenure in your new role. It's a harsh but valid lesson. The statistics are staggering: Over 64% of executives hired from outside the organization will not be highly successful in their new jobs (Bradt, Check, & Pedraza, 2009). Surprisingly, few school leaders receive any professional development on how to make the most effective transition to a new role and to how to diagnose the strengths and needs of an organization. This chapter outlines some of the best practices from both the corporate and nonprofit sectors to help give you some tools to hit the ground . . . listening.

One study (Smart, 1999) has suggested that over 50% of new CEOs fail within their first 2 years. "There just wasn't a good fit between the CEO and the organization" is often the reason given for the apparent lack of success. While there haven't been similar studies in the education world, anecdotally, there are frightening numbers of high potential, well prepared, good hearted people who are selected to lead schools who are marginally successful. Although few school executives are dismissed, many more are transferred or succumb to a burned-out, bitter, cynical tenure at that school before getting a chance to serve at a different school. In this chapter, we will outline specific steps to help you avoid derailment and ensure your success in the principalship. You'll learn common executive derailment factors, then analyze some tools, frameworks, and best practices to help you hit the ground listening in your new role.

Once You Have Been Chosen as the Leader

One best practice is to begin thinking about your new assignment at the time you are confirmed for your new role. You will generally have between 30 to 60 days to make the transition. Carve out time to plan cleaning and tidying up initiatives in your current role. Delegate what you can to others and document for your successor what you have been able to complete and what is still left undone. Then, spend time thinking about what you need to learn about your new organization. Peter Daly and Michael Watkins (2006) outline

1

a framework to more effectively make this transition. You should first think through the type of new organization you will lead. All principalships or superintendencies are not the same. Three of the most common types of organizations cited by Daly and Watkins include success-sustaining organizations, a realigned organization that focuses on new priorities, and organizations needing significant improvement. Each type of organization requires a different strategy to make the transition to effectiveness within the organization.

During your transition, you want to leverage your learning to ensure that you learn as much as you can about the school or district (technical learning), assess key sources of influence and coalitions (political learning), and understanding the norms, habits, and customs that shape the culture of your new organization (cultural learning).

1. At least 30 days prior to your first day on the job, review the most recent performance of the school or district you are taking over. Use the web to search for all information on your new school or district. You likely did this before your interview. If you are making an internal transfer to another role within the organization, take some time to analyze all the performance data that you can. Build up a base of facts that can help you get a bird's-eye view of the school or district.

2. Set up a meeting with the current incumbent principal or central office executive to get a better understanding of that person's perspective on the school improvement plan, district priorities, performance objectives, and any associated measures for those objectives. During this meeting, you also want to get this person's ideas on the key challenges facing the school, department, or district in the next 12, 24, and 36 months. You finally want to ask this person to identify the key stakeholders and their priorities. After the meeting, spend 15 minutes summarizing your notes and mapping out how the stakeholders are linked to each other and in what ways. You also want to spend a few minutes introducing yourself to your new secretary or lead secretary. You'll want to engage this person shortly in helping you set up meetings with these various stakeholders.

3. Set up a meeting with your future supervisor to get a sense of priorities. You want to cover questions with your new supervisor similar to those you discussed with the current incumbent principal. Be sure to ask your new supervisor about expected priorities and the type of organization you will be leading. Also, seek your supervisor's opinion on your direct reports. Take the time again after the meeting to map and confirm or modify your stakeholder network based on your conversations with your new supervisor and the current principal. You will use this map to identify critical internal and external alliances that can help you drive your agenda as you get into your new role.

Call your new secretary and request assistance to schedule meetings with these various stakeholders as well as your future direct reports prior to your first day on the job. These interviews should last about 20 minutes, giving you 10 minutes to catch your breath and summarize any notes. You should block out about an hour for your direct reports. You want to get a good sense of their priorities and capabilities during your time together. You can use the following sample questions as a springboard for your discussions (Coble, 2007).

The questions are framed for a principal for a new school. You can adapt these if you are in another role:

- ♦ What are our school's top 3 to 5 priorities?

- ♦ How do we plan to meet and achieve those priorities?

- ♦ What are your top 3 priorities? (You want to see how they match up with the school's priorities.)

- ♦ What are the 3 to 5 most important things we should preserve and keep doing here? Why?

- ♦ What are the top 3 things we need to change? Why?

- ♦ What do you most hope that I do?

- ♦ What are you most concerned that I might do?

- ♦ If you were in my shoes, what would you do first?

Take careful notes. Think like a researcher and synthesize what you have learned. These private sessions should be about establishing trust and adding context to the data. The conferences also communicate a willingness to listen and help inform your vision. It adds color to the data picture and provides insight into the school's culture.

Regardless of whether you are an insider or an outsider, you face the challenge of getting the people in your new organization to embrace you and buy into the vision that you have for your new organization. These lessons will substantially improve your chances for success in your new role.

Making Your Break Point

Mentally establish a clear "break point" where you decisively determine the tasks and projects you will complete in your current job and which tasks and projects will be left undone. Once you are selected for your new posting, you have two groups of people who will scramble for your time and attention. The person currently in your new role will want you to finish or approve pet projects and will seek a jump start to share perspectives on your own agenda. As you scramble to wind down in your current role and ramp up in the new, you need to think through the differences in the old and new jobs. The following chart in Figure 1.1 may help you crystallize your thinking: The first column delineates the major areas of focus. The second column ("old job") describes your priorities, your perception of your leadership team, constituents, and internal constituents. The third column ("new job") outlines your initial thoughts about your priorities, leadership team, and various constituencies. The fourth column gives you a chance to think through systematically how you plan to think, look, act, and behave differently in your new job, based in large part upon what you think about the needed priorities, your leadership team, and your constituencies. Finally, the last column gives you a chance to jot down questions you might have about your new job in terms of the four rows. You can use those questions as you navigate your transition.

Figure 1.1   Navigate Your Transition

Major areas of focus	"Old Job"	"New Job"	How you think, look, act, and behave differently	Questions you have about your new job
Priorities				
Leadership Team *School:* asst. principal, guidance, lead secretary *Central Office:* key subordinates				
External constituents *School:* PTA, athletic, arts, band boosters *Community:* chambers of commerce, business partners, and alliances				
Internal Constituents *School:* teachers, school leadership team *Central Office:* peer departments/divisions				

ST^RS: A Model for Organizational Transition

Daly and Watkins (2006) outline four major types of transitions that new leaders face. These transitions include start-ups, turnarounds, realignment, and sustaining success.

Start Up (S)

The two most frequent types of start-ups are opening a new school or a new division within central office. Start-ups share several challenges and opportunities:

1. Building organizational structures in the new school or organization

2. Developing a culture and informal controls

3. Bringing together multiple personalities, egos, and perspectives to weld them into a cohesive high- performing team

The biggest opportunity for you in start-up mode is the ability to create your own organization and team. There are fewer preconceived notions on what should and should not be done. The people that you bring on board are generally excited about the chance to start something new and to put their mark on a new organization. As the new principal and team leader, you have both the opportunity and the challenge to listen to each of your new team members. Some of them will have strong opinions about the "way we operate" at this school. It is important, however, to gain a deeper understanding of how all members view team processes and norms as you assume your new leadership role.

Turnaround (T^A)

In a turnaround situation, your toughest challenges will come in the areas of personnel and procedures. If your boss has not outlined your areas of focus during the selection and confirmation process, you need to quickly clarify your superintendent's expectations for you and the most pressing issues that need to be addressed.

Turnaround situations share some specific characteristics:

Denial or blame on the current state of affairs. The teachers, parents, and community know that there is a problem but there is little agreement on what the solution should be.

People who want to see change and those who are happy with the current state. Some people want the change for unselfish reasons while others see change as an opportunity to advance their particular cause. Others are very happy with the status quo because it takes them off the hook.

Ideally, your superintendent should introduce you to the faculty, share the issues from a district perspective, and discuss why you have been brought in to help. Having this conversation come from central office or the superintendent helps to set the stage for decisions in your first three months. Paradoxically, a turnaround is the type of assignment where you can make the biggest immediate positive impact. People understand the need for improvement and change even though they may not like it.

Realignment (R)

Schools in realignment have had past successes, but recent events demonstrate that changes must be made. Some examples of this may be a school that has been successful in the past but needs to change due to external events, such as redistricting. Another example of realignment may result from internal events, such as outmoded instructional programs that used to work but are no longer effective, or were dependent upon certain teachers who are no longer there.

Principals appointed to schools that are undergoing a realignment will have different challenges. Your role as a leader in a realignment situation is to spend more time listening at first and then helping people understand the need for a change. You have to spend significant time at the beginning educating your different stakeholders about the challenges facing the school and helping them internalize the need for change. A frequent mistake occurs when a new school executive arrives with a mandate for change but lacks the necessary support from the faculty, staff, and community.

Sustaining Success (S)

This type of leadership challenge occurs when a school or organization has been high performing and the staff sees little reason to improve. The leader in this type of transition does a lot more behind the scenes working to building coalitions and alliances. In the beginning, you should spend time listening and learning about what makes the organization perform well, under what conditions, and in what areas. What you learn will pinpoint areas for improvement and help you know how to react if performance starts to suffer. You will also gain insight into political coalitions, alliances, and outside resources to call when needed in the future.

Make the Most of the Your First 90 Days

You now should have an initial idea of the type of organization you are stepping into. Your next step is to make the most of your first 3 months. Your actions in your first 90 days will set the stage for your leadership agenda.

Agree on Your Mandate

You should know your superintendent's (or your immediate supervisor's) views on the most important issues to be addressed and how to get commitment to make progress on them. The most effective bosses will put metrics in place to evaluate the progress. Your role is to ensure that your boss's expectations are realistic. It is important to have a shared definition of what success looks like and your decision-making boundaries around key areas like finance, moving people around/transferring them, or if need be, demoting or dismissing them.

Frontload Your Learning

You should focus upon three main types of learning when you begin to make your transition: technical, political, and cultural.

- ◆ *Technical learning:* Understand the nature and key success factors of student achievement in your school.

  ◇ What instructional programs and curriculum programs are being used in your school? How effective is each program?

  ◇ How are they measured?

  ◇ How long have these programs been in place?

If you are moving to a central office role, technical learning includes understanding the rhythm and cycle of different activities that occur during the school year. For instance, in human resources, there is a distinct recruiting season, an induction season, a performance review season, and a rehiring/termination season.

♦ *Political Learning*: Understand the various formal and informal networks.

◊ Who are participants in different informal alliances and coalitions?

◊ Which groups are the current "power players"?

◊ Which groups are aspiring to be the next group of power players?

Power, whether used for good or bad, is a reality in organizational life. Ignore it at your peril. You need to know the constituents, both internal and external to the school, to whom others pay attention.

♦ *Cultural Learning*: Understand the important informal processes, myths, and beliefs.

◊ What does the school do to connect, reflect, and celebrate?

◊ What rituals, traditions, and ceremonies are important?

Recent research suggests that positive school culture promotes school achievement and effectiveness. You have the opportunity to shape the culture of your school, but first, you need to diagnose the current culture. Deal and Peterson (2009) suggests some tactics to understand the history of the school:

♦ Review old newsletters, faculty meeting agendas, achievement results, graduation plans, and school improvement plans.

♦ Talk to faculty, staff, business partners, central office executives, and parents to see what previous principals were like, how the staff interacted, and what major events (if any) were central to shaping people's views, attitudes, and values.

♦ Ask each person to list six adjectives that describe the school. After you have completed the interviews, put the words on sticky notes and rearrange them to see if any themes emerge (positive or negative).

STEEP Model

Another model for analyzing the environment is the STEEP (Social, Technological, Economic, Educational, and Political) analysis (Kyler, 2003). This analysis (See Figure 1.2) gives you a way to see what forces are likely to help or hinder you as you drive your agenda. As you analyze each aspect in the STEEP framework, answer five questions:

1. Whose support do I need?

2. What do these individuals want and why?

3. What style of influence worked well in the past?

4. What will likely work now (data, precedent, rewards/threats, empowering, or a vision of the future)?

5. Will your preferred leadership style work here? If not, who can you enlist to complement the way you work to help achieve your agenda?

FIGURE 1.2   STEEP Analysis

STEEP Analysis	Current	Historical
Social (how well people work with each other, the informal norms of collegiality, performance, and improvement)		
Technological (frequency and type of technology used both in the classroom and administratively)		
Economic (whether the community is growing/shrinking; experiencing job growth/loss)		
Educational (student achievement by subgroups)		
Political (relationship between previous incumbent in your role and various stakeholders; relationship between the superintendent and the board/community)		

ID Crucial Allies

You also may look at the engagement levels of each of your stakeholders. Figure 1.3 gives you an example of how you can analyze your various stakeholders. Take each row and analyze how supportive each group is about you in your new role. Obviously you have your superintendent's strong support. Yet, if other groups had lobbied for another candidate, they may be neutral, moderately against, or strongly against you in your new role. Systematically analyze whether you need their support early in your transition. If so, determine what you plan to do to increase their support of you in the last column.

Weld Your Team

When you transition to your new organization, you have two major tasks in welding your team together: determining who will be on your team and helping them be successful.

Determine who will be on your team: When a new person comes on board, some people stay and some people move on to other organizations. The first time this happens to you, you start to wonder, "Am I being too harsh or too loose in my requirements of

FIGURE 1.3   ID Crucial Allies

	Strongly Against	Moderately Against	Neutral	Moderately Supportive	Strongly Supportive	Plan to Reduce Gaps (if you choose to)
Superintendent						
Your immediate manager						
PTA/PTO president						
Business partners						
Athletic booster president						
Band booster president						
School improvement team						
Teacher union president						
School board						
Noncertified staff						

my team? Why is this person leaving me?" One recent research study in the private sector suggests that about 15% leave within a year of a new manager. If the person is promoted from inside the organization, that figure drops to 11%. If the organization has underperformed, upward of 20% of the key leadership team leaves within the first year (Coyne, 2008).

As you meet with your team members, you want to determine if they are the right people for the team and the challenges you face. Ciampa and Watkins (2008) suggest the following questions that we have adapted for education settings:

- Have they stayed up to date on current instructional trends and issues?

- Do they have an organizational perspective, or do they suffer from paro-chial self-interest?

- Can they cooperate with each other, and have they been expected to do so in the past?

- Do they work well as a team or only when there is a crisis?

- How is the group (and specific individuals) perceived by the people under them—are they feared, respected, or ignored?

- Do their skills complement each other's skills, and do they complement your skills?

Help them be successful with you: It is important to be transparent about your hot buttons and how you work best. Share your style preferences with them on areas such as the following:

- Do you prefer oral or written information?

- Do you prefer formal or informal titles? Some principals like to be referred to as Mr., Mrs., Ms., or Dr. Others prefer a first-name basis when not with students.

- Do you prefer to be involved early in the process? Do you want to have a recommendation presented to you in a yes/no format? Or, do you want three options with advantages and disadvantages of each option laid out? Does it matter in different parts of the school (curriculum and instruction, operations, finance) or across the board? This should not mean that they surprise you with anything, but as you see in our delegation chapter, you need to leverage their efforts.

- How should they disagree with you? Can they disagree with you publicly? Do you prefer private discussions of disagreements? Can they push back on some of your ideas, or are your ideas firm once communicated?

- Do you prefer facts and data or stories to illustrate points?

- What should *not* come as a surprise to you?

- What is your threshold for when subordinates should inform you in advance? One principal we knew outlined specifics across nine different aspects of schoolwork with the questions above (operations, finance, disci-pline, teachers, students, parents, external partners, board of education, and superintendent). You don't need to necessarily write this out in that level of specificity, but it is good to think it through. It leverages your time and helps develop your team.

Early Wins Create Momentum

You should have a pretty hefty set of notes by this time. Go back and identify the themes that appear. Are there any themes that you can easily resolve? If so, attack those themes early. You want to set the tone that you have listened to your different stakeholders. You should have a series of themes that you categorize along one axis with ease of implementation and the other axis as a timeframe, as Figure 1.4 illustrates.

+ **Easy to Implement and Short-Term:** Those themes and actions should be implemented immediately—within the first 30 days of your tenure, if possible. You want to demonstrate you have heard and acted upon the concerns and suggestions from your stakeholders.

+ **Easy to Implement and Long-Term:** These actions and themes can be delegated to a committee, with your monitoring to ensure completion. Your delegation of these themes demonstrates that you are a leader comfortable with the skills and talents of your team and that you expect these to be completed within a certain block of time.

+ **Hard to Implement and Short-Term:** Assuming these themes are congruent with what you have as your priorities, you need to spend your initial time in this quadrant of themes and activities. You should carefully consider what needs to be done, when it needs to be done, what resources you are willing to put into it, and what specific measurements you have to demonstrate success.

+ **Hard to Implement and Long-Term:** Themes in this quadrant will need additional time to educate your different stakeholders on the need to change and focus upon this problem. You'll spend your first 6 months analyzing different aspects of these issues to ensure that you have the data to support the crux of these issues.

By the end of the 6 months, you should have made substantial progress in addressing some of the issues and challenges outlined by your boss in your initial meeting. You should be minding your priorities and keeping your focus on the critical few, rather than the myriad other activities that can mire you in the activity trap. Your energy is focused on your priorities, you have categorized your issues into four "buckets" and you have an action plan for each of these buckets. You're ready to align the skills and talents of your leadership team and your school improvement team into a high performing team.

FIGURE 1.4   New Challenge Themes

Easy to Implement and Long-Term Delegate these to a committee and monitor for completion.	**Hard to Implement and Long-Term** Set up a timeline and spend your time educating your different stakeholders about these needs.
Easy to Implement and Short-Term Act on these first.	**Hard to Implement and Short-Term** Set up a timeline and spend your energy here.

Derailers

Researchers have analyzed the behaviors that contribute to senior executives either derailing or being marginally successful in the executive suite (Coble 2007; Daly & Watkins, 2006; Dotlich & Cairo, 2003; Lombardo & Eichinger, 1989). One model you might use is a four-category analysis of derailment factors (Ludeman & Erlandson, 2006). Many of these behaviors serve executives well in moderation but, when taken to excess, create a dark side that can contribute to one's downfall. Ludeman and Erlandson (2006) surveyed over 1,500 male and female business executives and suggest four categories of leaders whose positive attributes have the potential for derailment. See Figure 1.5.

Dotlitch outlines some derailers that tend to trip up even the most effective leaders at one time or another. Take a look at them and assess yourself on a 1 to 5 scale (1=*never describes me* to 5=*frequently describes me*).

Arrogance: "You're right and everybody else is wrong." While you need to be confident, arrogance is a blinding belief that you and you alone are right. This is especially acute in two situations:

♦ when you have been asked to come in to clean up a mess

♦ in your first executive role

Many times, leaders who have this derailer operate under stress and become too insulated, bringing in only people who agree with what they say, leading to disaster.

Your Self Rating _____

Melodrama: "You have to grab the center of attention." Charisma is frequently over-rated. In an attempt to achieve what some refer to as "executive presence," your exaggerated emotion when trying to make a point ends up distracting people. Your showboating makes the nonverbal point that other people's ideas are not wanted or

FIGURE 1.5 Possible Derailers

Category	Advantages	Derailers
Commander (*Gen. George Patton or Jack Welch*)	Winning battles, making decisions, decisive, energetic	Domineering, intimidating, uncontrollable
Visionaries (*Richard Branson*)	Inspirational, motivational, charismatic, outsized goals, ambitious, creative	Overconfident, unrealistic, defensive
Strategists (*Michael Eisner or Donald Rumsfeld*)	Very methodical, process oriented, intelligent, objective, analytical	Smug, pretentious, arrogant, unemotional
Executors (*Sam Walton*)	Disciplined and relentless, timeless, demanding	Impatient, inflexible, unreasonable, unappreciative

needed. If you have a tendency to melodrama, meetings can quickly degenerate into low theater and tragic comedy. Your subordinates think the only way to make a point is to stomp and throw a fit. Is that the kind of meeting that you want to lead?

Your Self Rating _____

Volatility: *"Your mood shifts suddenly and unpredictably."* People frequently remark about leaders having "high energy." This is a strength, yet when you are unpredictable in your comments or mood, you'll find people who are tentative when talking to you. They may be trying to gauge your mood and temperament during your conversation. One sure sign you are volatile occurs when you overhear people asking your secretary for a sense of your mood before coming in to see you.

Your Self Rating _____

Risk Aversion: *"The next decision you make may be your first."* Many people have heard of analysis by paralysis. When you think and rethink before making a decision because you are afraid of making the wrong decision, you suffer from risk aversion. You've heard of managers who ask for one more study, one more task force, one more look at the data in a different way. The result is meaningless action rather than moving forward, and the very problem you sought to avoid by getting more information becomes an urgent issue and spirals out of control.

Your Self Rating _____

Habitual distrust: *"You focus on the negatives."* You should maintain a healthy skepticism about problems that could go wrong at your school, for example, angry parents, potential lawsuits, child safety, and security. Healthy skepticism involves realism and realistic assessment of the risks and mitigating them. Yet, if you continually focus upon the negatives and what could go wrong, you'll create a toxic work environment. You'll notice this when your direct reports act highly defensive over each issue and their recommendations. You'll also see this when you have difficulty forging or maintaining alliances with outside groups. If your outside groups tend to shy away from you, they may be giving you a clear signal that your focus upon what could go wrong is becoming an issue.

Your Self Rating _____

Aloofness: *"You disengage and disconnect."* Silent Sam (or Samantha) is a caricature of a school leader that never leaves the office, keeps the door closed throughout the day, and leaves the cocoon only to see a few trusted subordinates. Unfortunately, these executives frequently got to their current roles because of their superior technical skills. Their people skills have atrophied to the extent of being nonexistent. If people ask "Who is the principal here?" that is a sure sign that you are being aloof and unavailable to help people with answers to their questions.

Your Self Rating _____

Mischievousness: *"Rules are really only suggestions."* Many school executives agree that bureaucracy stifles innovation and increased performance. You might have heard of schools and districts with calcified procedures and regulations. Yet, when you throw out provocative ideas just to be different without helping others execute the most promising ideas to improve your school, you risk being labeled as either a provocateur, scatterbrained, or eccentric.

Your Self Rating _____

Passive resistance: *"Your silence implies agreement with the decision."* You should consciously and deliberately signify your agreement with a course of action. If you fail to signify your concerns early in the process, you run the risk of confusing and angering teachers, colleagues, and community members by your comments later on. If the course of action does not give the anticipated results and you then criticize the idea, you will lose your credibility. Dotlitch suggests that a test for passive resistance is whether you see people moving from confusion to anger to cynicism. Your unwillingness to walk the talk by failing to make your real views on certain issues known is another sign of this derailer.

Your Self Rating _____

Perfectionism: *"Get the little things right even if the big things go wrong."* You've seen others who refuse to delegate anything to anybody else. These presumed "masters of the universe" think nobody can complete the task as well as them. Unfortunately, past success can breed future failure. Successfully using those skills (usually technical skills) as an individual contributor can blind people to what the requirements of their new role entails. Perfectionism can easily create a self-defeating and rapidly descending "doom loop" when the leader does not focus on the key success factors in the new role.

Your Self Rating _____

Eagerness to please: *"Winning the popularity contest matters most."* A school executive's job is lonely. It's normal to want to be liked, yet you run the risk of this derailer when you make decisions based upon how people will like you. Teams suffer and fall apart if their leader does not support them publicly and privately after members have successfully completed a controversial assignment. Another symptom of this derailer occurs when a school executive fails to confront a person when they are out of line. Have you heard somebody mention that nobody knows where the school executive stands? This is a third symptom of the derailer.

Your Self Rating _____

After you have rated yourself, look at one or two areas that you think you might want to focus on to help you avoid derailing and improve as a leader by better understanding your strengths and areas of growth. Goldsmith suggests that changing the way you are and act is not impossible, but it is sustained difficult work (2007). Your best bet in the meantime is to understand your strengths and understand that if you overuse your strengths, they can become weaknesses. You should consider finding people on your team whose strengths match your weaknesses. Teams with members who have complementary skills are the most cohesive and effective teams.

2
Finding Time for Instructional Leadership

Have you ever heard a school executive say, "I don't have to work that hard. The principalship is a pretty easy job." In fact, you frequently hear the contrary: a litany of being overworked with a constant bombardment of innumerable daily actions and tasks. School executives never have enough time in the day. Many principals report that they get over 100 daily e-mails. School executives must juggle e-mails with voice mail, school meetings, central office meetings, and the informal "Hey, Boss—you got a minute?" conversations that can take 30 minutes. Where will you find time to do everything that needs to get done? You begin processing e-mails but you get sidetracked. A student comes in needing counseling. A teacher wants to get your opinion on a letter she is preparing to send out. All of these items by themselves are important, yet you feel that you never get anything done.

Part of this issue comes from the work itself. Kent Peterson (2001) noted that principals have between 400 and 500 interactions on a daily basis. To put this in perspective, your 2-minute conversation with your secretary may qualify as a lengthy conversation!

As school executives, you are also in a helping profession. You received your promotions because you were a terrific individual contributor. Many principals fit this profile. They started as teachers and were good (if not great) teachers. They were able to differentiate instruction to meet various student needs. These future school executives had good rapport with parents, and they volunteered for additional tasks to help the school. A mentor (usually the teacher's principal) took an interest in them and encouraged them to get the necessary credentials to become a school principal. Once credentialed, they soon became an assistant principal. During this transition, the fledgling assistant principal vowed to be a "teachers' principal" and not to hide behind a closed door. When they got into the role of assistant principal, they found that they could not do all that they were tasked with completing during that mythical 40- or even 50-hour work week. So, they stayed late, worked late hours after school and the mythical 40-hour workweek had an additional 10 hours per week tacked on to the end.

When they became a principal, they entered a new dimension of being overwhelmed. They stayed late, an extra 2 hours per day; they took work home, and continued to work after their children and spouse went to bed. They awoke early the next morning to attempt to "catch up" on administrative work that keeps piling up. The 50-hour workweek becomes 60, 70, and even 80 hours during a 7-day span. One principal noted that trying to catch up on e-mail was akin to the arcade game, "Whack-A-Mole." ©

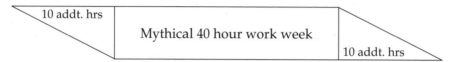

Although you may never return to this mythical 40-hour workweek, we will suggest some tools you can use to move back to a 50-hour workweek. School executives use these with success to clear their desks, reduce clutter, and regain their focus on instructional leadership. These tools also help the executive manage processes to keep the school running effectively. Regaining control involves three main categories of time management: collecting, processing, and action.

Smart Time Management: Collecting

Many school executives (from assistant principal to superintendent) get tangled up when they try to multitask. Rubinstein, Meyer, and Evans (2001) found that multitaskers were less efficient and effective when they had to shift mental gears, especially with unfamiliar tasks. You have to maintain a laserlike focus on one thing at a time. This focus can last a few seconds or a couple of hours.

Many executives are bombarded with questions, requests, and action items. These action items come from phone messages, quick conversations on the way from the parking lot to the school door, faculty meetings, department or grade-level meetings, e-mails, and requests from central office. You will not always be worrying about where you took notes if you avoid making them on scraps of paper or scribbling in the margins and on the back of napkins and instead employ a minimal number of collection tools or "holding places."

Each of your impromptu meetings, conversations, e-mails, and voice mail messages may require action. You also get ideas that awaken you in the middle of the night. You get ideas from articles, magazines, and professional journals. All of these are opportunities to capture thoughts and impressions.

David Allen (2002) suggests that you should resolve an issue or item if you can do so in 2 minutes or less. If you cannot, you need to use various collection tools to collect notes, voice mails, and action items from your various scheduled and impromptu meetings.

Phone Messages

One collection tool is how you collect phone messages. Whether your secretary takes your messages or people come directly to your voice mail, it is important to keep a log of the phone calls in one place. Those small pink slips of paper can easily get buried under a pile on your desk. If possible, have an administrative assistant, receptionist, or your secretary take all of your calls, rather than simply putting callers into your voice mail. Have your secretary keep all calls on either a commercially developed pad or adapt the call log in Figure 2.1.

FIGURE 2.1   Phone Log

Status	Who	Number	RE:	Notes

Many principals and assistant principals have moved to individual phone logs in the office. They print out many copies of this (or a similar) form on a different color of paper for each person, spiral bind the blank phone log, and give them to the school reception-ist or secretary. When a person calls for either the principal or assistant principal, the receptionist writes it down on the phone log, filling in the "who," "number," and "RE:" columns. When the principal and assistant principal comes in from classroom visits or out-of-office meetings, they pick up their phone log, ask the receptionist if there are any urgent messages or "energized" parents, and then begin returning the phone calls. The first column "status" indicates whether the call has been completed. Once the school leader initiates the call, she places a dash (–) in the status cell. Once the call is completed, change the dash to a plus (+).

After the school leader goes through the phone log, she returns it to the receptionist and moves on to the next item on her daily schedule or agenda. If the parent returns the call once again, the receptionist puts a circle around the dash to indicate that the parent returned the call.

We think having a person, rather than an automated message, answer your phone has a number of advantages. The secretary can screen, prioritize the call, and calm an angry caller. We've all been switched to voice mail when we wanted to talk to a live human voice. When we get voice mail, it makes us even angrier. The same is true with your callers. An effective secretary can tell the caller where you are ("She's out in the building visiting classrooms; she should be back in about an hour. May I take a message?"), gauge the intensity of the call, and give you a heads-up when you return ("Call Mrs. Smith immediately. She is very upset about an incident in Ms. Young's class yesterday.").

A call log gives you additional time to make the callbacks in the order and priority that you decide. On the other hand, if you go back to your office to listen to each voice mail message, it may take you up to five times as long as simply reading the notes section for each call. More efficient is to take the phone log, make the return calls, and log when you completed the call. The time you save by simply having your secretary answer your calls can also reinforce with the caller your focus on classroom learning ("She's observing teachers this morning. May I tell her you called?").

Batching Similar Items

One strategy attributed to Andy Grove (1999) is the concept of batching similar items. This allows you to complete the items more efficiently. Rather than returning each phone call when you get a chance, or processing your e-mail at random times throughout the day, consider instead the idea of batching all of your similar activities together. At the beginning of the day, spend 30 minutes processing your e-mail and returning phone calls. Then check again at midday and at the end of the day.

Meeting Notes

Many principals take copious notes. Having an effective way to keep these notes collected will help you avoid getting overwhelmed or having action items fall through the cracks. You'll quickly see the value of having a way to keep action items organized if you miss a budget deadline for spending this year's funds. You might use portfolio pads, a bound journal to take meeting notes, or 3 x 5-inch cards to capture those ideas and notes taken on the run.

The key to using the portfolio pad successfully is to use it not only to capture notes from meetings, but also to capture action items that you need to complete. Reduce collection points by using a new sheet of paper for each day. You then have an instant running log of what you have done during any day. The portfolio pad is especially good for those who want to drop the sheet of paper in a file folder in preparation for each project or meeting. The disadvantage to this method is that if you forget the file folder during the meeting, you don't have any of your notes.

An alternative that other school executives use is a hard-bound journal to take meeting notes and jot down action items. You can have a new page for every day with meeting notes. Other school executives use the left side for phone calls and action items and the right side as a notes page for meetings during the day. Like the portfolio model, the hard bound journal has the advantage keeping all of your notes in one place, but the notes are organized chronologically, not by the individual project or meeting.

3 x 5-inch Cards

There are places where you have forgotten or don't want to carry your notebook. Instead of trying to write on a scrap of paper, carry around a few 3 x 5-inch index cards, which are perfect for collecting information, ideas, and actions from quick meetings. If you get a question from a parent, a student, or a faculty member, you can jot it down on the card. To ensure that you don't drop the ball, put just one idea, comment, or action on a single card, rather than combining a number of unrelated items together. The additional step will help as you process the information later in the day.

Magazine Articles

You receive several articles and magazines each month. You may think, "Sometime I may need this," as a rationale to keep these magazines. You can reduce your clutter by taking a look at the table of contents for each magazine. Are there any articles that interest you? If not, throw the magazine away after pulling out the table of contents pages. If there is an article that interests you, tear out the article, staple it on the corner, and put it in a file folder that holds articles for future reading when you had some "wait" time. Wait time includes time waiting for an appointment, waiting for a conference call, or during large meetings where people have a history of being long-winded. Keep the table of contents only if you cannot access the journal online. You can digitize this by looking at the website for the magazine and creating a PDF of the table of contents, which you keep in an electronic file folder—one for each trade journal and magazine.

A Ravine? Or a Bridge? Using a Smart File System

Bridges help you get from one side of the ravine to the other side without losing any of your cargo. Similarly, we use the idea of a bridge to move from the collecting phase to the processing and action phases. Once you have reduced your collection points, you have two processing decisions to make. The first decision is: should you take action on this message or item? If it is an information item only, you simply have a second decision: delete it or put in a reference file. Reference files can be either a smart paper filing system or electronic files on your network or computer.

What 43 File Folders Can Do for You

If you want to clear your desk of clutter, you have to have a place to put it. Many people mistakenly think that they know where everything is in their various piles. Yet, frequently, they run late on getting critical tasks done or they misplace a report they have to file on a specific date. One tool to reduce this problem is emptying a file drawer in your desk and creating 43 hanging file folders, which you might think of as a three-dimensional calendar. The 43-file folder concept is made up of 31 daily files, labeled 1 through 31 and 12 monthly file folders for January through December (hence the name). The concept is deceptively simple. Determine which day you need to complete the task on a piece of paper, and put it in that day's file folder. Pull out the folder for each day and complete the action items. Mail or reports that require a response should be placed in one of the 43 folders.

If you receive a report due on the 23rd, 13 days out, simply put the document in the folder labeled 22. You can relax knowing that you will take care of the report before the deadline .

Let's consider a few more examples. If you know that you have to create next year's budget starting in October, put a note to remind yourself to start this in your October file folder. If you have to start thinking about summer school in January and buy new computers in March, put those items in the respective file folder for the month. Here's a key tip: ONLY put the items within the next 31 days in the 1-31 file folder. If something has to be done more than 31 days out, put it in the monthly file folder. At the beginning of each month, pull out the items in that month's folder and file them in one of the 1-31 file folders. Many people devote a file drawer on the left or right side of their desk to keep the 43 folders easily accessible.

Key People and Meeting Files

You probably have specific people with whom you work on a frequent basis. Some likely roles within school are assistant principal(s), financial secretary, guidance counselor/dean of student services, Special Education chair, and grade level or department chairs. You may also have the PTA president, athletics director, band director, and your superintendent (or whomever you report to). Create a file folder for each of them to drop notes and things that you want to talk about when you meet them. When you have a meeting with the individual, you have your quick list of possible agenda items.

Many principals also extend this idea to key meetings as well. They create a file folder for faculty meetings and for their monthly principal meetings with their colleagues. The main idea is to have your information at ready access when you need it without trying to keep it all in your head.

Smart Time Management: Processing

Here's a strategy that has worked well for school executives who process their tasks two or three times daily. It starts at the end of the afternoon, just before going home.

- ◆ Process your e-mail and return as many of phone calls as you are able to do.

- ◆ Spend 5 minutes reviewing the day's activities and what you were unable to accomplish during the day that needs to be moved forward to the following day.

- ◆ Look at the projects that have an action due for the following day.

- ◆ Finally, write down the top 3 things that you need to accomplish during the next day.

This 5-minute routine at the end of the day helps you clear your head, focus on what you want to accomplish tomorrow, and allows you to decompress on your drive home.

The next morning, you might follow a set routine:

- ◆ Check voice mail messages, write them down, and *don't* return any calls unless they are urgent (or from the superintendent).

- ◆ Take a quick scan of your e-mail (do a sort on the "From" field) to look only at urgent e-mails or ones from the superintendent. Key point: Don't respond to any e-mails at this time, unless they are urgent. Let's face it: There are few e-mails that require immediate response. If there is an emergency with a student or a teacher, you obviously resolve that issue, but the vast majority of the e-mails can wait for processing.

- ◆ You're then visible in the halls or in the parking lot talking to students, teachers, and community members as they come in to school.

- ◆ Once school has started, have a 5-minute stand-up meeting with your leadership team (assistant principal and lead secretary to get a sense of the current issues for the day.

- ◆ Tackle your to-do list that you created last evening, trying to take care of the number one item on your list. That number one item could be analysis of data, conducting three observations, or completing a report. Whatever it is, try to gain momentum by moving as far on your number one project as possible. If for some reason, you are unable to complete your number one item, go on to your second item and get as much of that item completed as possible.

Once you have completed your first item, you can move on to item #2 or start to process the daily e-mails and paperwork that comes across your desk or those items that were placed in your daily folder from the 43 file folders.

The OHIO Method

As you process items, ask, Can I actually "do something" with this item? You might follow the dictum: If you can get something done in 2 minutes or less, then do it now (Allen, 2002). If you cannot do anything with the item, you then ask, Can I delete it or must I keep it for reference? To avoid being a packrat, ask yourself, "Will somebody else be able to pull this from a reference file? If so, why do I need to keep this for myself?"

If the message or item does require action, then you have three other choices: delegate it to another person (more on this later in chapter 2), do it now, or defer the item. How do you make that decision? Think "OHIO in 2 minutes."

OHIO is an acronym for the phrase "only handle it once." Whenever possible, you want to handle the item one time. This is simple arithmetic. Let's assume you have 50 items each day. You take action on about 20 and you defer the other 30 to the following day. The next day, you have 50 more plus the 30 you didn't act on yesterday. You look at each one of those 80 and you take action on about 20, look at the 30 from the previous day and you now have 60 items to act on. By the end of the week, you have looked at your first 30 four times with a total number of 450 items that you still need to act on. It is much better to think "Read, Decide. Read, Decide. Read, Decide." If you can take care of the item in 2 minutes or less, do it now. If you want, get a timer and set it for 2 minutes per item time frame and see how many items you can resolve in 2 minutes.

If you have decided that the message or item will take more than 2 minutes, you need to have strategies that will help organize items for later. Three bridge tools that are especially helpful are the 43 file folders discussed earlier, individual file folders for your key people, and key meeting file folders.

You can self-monitor how many times you handle a piece of paper by putting a dot in the top right hand corner of each incoming item. Each time you handle that particular piece of paper, put an additional dot on it. If you end up with three dots, you are procrastinating on what to do with that item. Take 5 to 10 minutes and decide once and for all what you want to do with that document.

D4: Delete, Delegate, Do, Defer

With all noncritical items, you can use a process called **D4: Delete, Delegate, Do, Defer**. This frees you to intentionally focus on your top priorities rather than attempting to address all the small items that come up during the day.

For an example of how this work, let's look at reducing the amount of time sorting through e-mails.

♦ **DELETE.** Ask: *"Can I delete this? What's the worst that can happen if I delete it?"*

If you can delete it, it goes to the e-mail trash can. If it cannot be deleted, then move to the next "D".

♦ **DELEGATE.** Ask: *"I know that I can do this, but is there someone to whom I can delegate this item?"*

Forward the e-mail to that person. Make a note in your tracking folder if it is important enough to track.

♦ **DO:** If you cannot delete or delegate it, then **do** it.

Respond to the message if it takes 2 minutes or less. That forces you to jot off a quick reply on the e-mail. Most people only want a brief response. They know that you don't have time for a lengthy epistle. In fact, one rule of thumb on e-mailing is that if your response requires a person to scroll, it's too long.

♦ **DEFER.** Finally, if the e-mail will take more than 2 minutes to respond, **defer** by moving the item to a folder called "Action."

This e-mail folder is for the items that you will handle later in the day. You can also put the item in your list of various tasks and actions you track.

Tips on Managing E-mail

We've listed some tips from school executives on how they manage e-mail. Process e-mail for about 30 minutes two or three times a day. Create three e-mail folders using Manage Folders, on the toolbar next to your inbox. These three folders are Action, Follow-Up, and Processed.

♦ The **Action** folder holds e-mails that require action from you sometime in the next 48 hours. These items take more than 2 minutes to complete.

♦ The **Follow-Up** folder is for e-mails you have delegated and need follow-up. When you e-mail the person, add your name to the "cc" line, and save that e-mail to the Follow-Up folder. Check that file folder weekly and delete the message once they have responded. Send another e-mail or schedule a conference if the task is still outstanding.

♦ The **Processed** folder contains almost all of those e-mails you want to keep as a reference for some future use. Take advantage of the category feature in most e-mail programs. You can "tag" an e-mail with multiple categories, such as "reference," "PTA/PTO," "Superintendent," "Central Office," and so on. You can easily sort and filter your e-mails using tags/categories to quickly retrieve the e-mail you are looking for.

Your Calendar Should Reflect Your Priorities

Nothing reflects your priorities like your daily calendar. If you don't block out time for your priorities, they get crowded out. Linda Cowan, a principal in Anson County, NC, shared a strategy that clearly outlines her priorities. She blocks out Tuesday and

FIGURE 2.2   Calendar Priorities

Time	Monday	Tuesday	Wednesday	Thursday	Friday
AM	Classroom visits	Paperwork and processing		Paperwork and processing	
Mid Day			Classroom visits		
PM					Classroom visits

Thursday mornings to process her paperwork and mail. She leaves Monday, Wednesday, and Friday free and blocked out a 3-hour block of time on each of those days for observations and visiting classrooms. One way to set up your weekly schedule based on Linda's wisdom is listed in Figure 2.2.

One other calendaring tip is to schedule only half of the day. This allows you to move and shift things around if the day gets hairy. If you are responsible for instructional leadership but you don't create any time to actively engage in instructional leadership, you will be behind the power curve and will be constantly trying to catch up.

Share Your Calendar

Your secretary can serve as an invaluable partner to help you leverage your time. Try giving a copy of your calendar to your lead secretary each day or week. Whether you use a paper calendar or keep it on a computer network, it is vital that the secretary knows your priorities and where you are during the day. One school executive shared this anecdote on what not to do:

> My first principalship was a case where I was brought in to help turn around the school. One of my rookie mistakes was keeping what I was doing and my calendar close to me and not letting my secretary know where I was. One day, I got a phone call from the assistant superintendent who wanted some additional information on a grant proposal that I had submitted to her. This was a very substantial amount of money, and I had worked hard to get the grant ready for submission. The deadline was 5 p.m. that day. When she called the school, she asked the secretary if I was available. My secretary's truthful response was, "I don't know where he is or even if he is in the building." Needless to say, we didn't get the grant, I was coached on how important it is to keep my secretary informed of where I was, and I started sharing my calendar with my secretary and my two assistant principals.

Monitoring Your Success, Weekly Review, and Braggables

Monitoring progress is critical to achieving success. You also need some way to loop back around at the end of the week to make sure that nothing has fallen through the cracks. You may think you are too busy to do this, but this discipline of keeping a record of accomplished goals will be quite valuable when compiling successes for your performance review or when you decide to dust off your resume.

Each week, block out about an hour on your calendar to go back through all of your collection points and action notes to ensure that you haven't forgotten anything. Process each item and if it takes less than 2 minutes, then get it done and out of the way. Michael Hyatt (www.michaelhyatt.com) has a systematized weekly discipline. He reviews the following seven areas to make sure that he is caught up on his priorities:

- Any loose papers

- Notes taken with different collection points (journals, 3 x 5-cards, etc.)

- The current week's calendar—review to see if there was anything you missed.

- Upcoming week—identify activities that may require a large block of time

- Action lists/to-do lists

- Follow-up lists

- Wishes list. (This lists all the things Hyatt "might" be interested in. He takes a look at this weekly to see if anything has bubbled up to move these ideas to an action list.

David Maister (2003) notes that a critical second part of the weekly review is to outline what you have accomplished by taking 10 minutes to review what you have accomplished during the week. You might create a simple word processing document that looks like Figure 2.3.

The date and accomplishment are self-explanatory. You want to have a reference column to refer back to when you are asked to give specifics about what you accomplished. The right-hand column is a terrific reflection tool for you to reflect on what you learned from the accomplishment.

FIGURE 2.3 Weekly Accomplishments

Date	Accomplishment	Reference	What I learned

Smart Time Management: Take Action

All the processing in the world will not help you with your time management if you don't take action. Many school and business executives have been guilty of putting everything in place and writing everything down, rather than actually completing items. In the next sections, we discuss identifying priorities, managing large projects, and delegation—all characteristics of effective leaders.

Focus on Priorities

One of the traits that Stephanie Winston found in her analysis of time management strategies of top executives is a laser focus upon the task at hand (2004). She points out that almost all managers and executives live in a very fragmented world and that the most effective leaders become comfortable in the chaos. They chunked their top three priorities, yet kept the remainder of their day open to whittle down other items that came up during the day, whether it was a drop in meeting or processing e-mail. Winston found that the key for one executive was keeping her focus upon the task at hand, even if the focus was for 15 seconds. It was like a laser pulsing on and off. This laserlike focus mind-set allowed the executive to adapt to the constantly changing number of interactions that occurred during the day.

Ask "What Justifies Your Being on the Payroll?"

Peter Drucker asked the question "What justifies your being on the payroll?" (2006). The first role of the executive, he notes, is to **determine what the job requires, not what you want to do.** The second role of the executive is to make **what the job requires the executive's top priority.** The third role of the executive is to **know where his or her time goes.** Oftentimes, they do not match up.

Unfortunately, many school executives haven't thought through what the job requires. They either treat their job as a school executive as identical to other school executive roles (all assistant principalships and principalships are the same), or they apply for a promotion, because they have been encouraged to do so, but without fully understanding what the particular role entails. Two principalships in the same school district, at the same level, with similar demographics may have radically different needs. One may require the principal to be a cheerleader and motivator of a staff that has a great deal of talent but has low morale. The other principalship may require the principal to turn the school around. The job description does not always capture all of the requirements of a particular position and school.

Try this exercise:

- List all of the tasks and meetings you had in the past 2 weeks.

- Group all of these tasks and meetings into 10 different priorities.

- Filter these tasks and meetings down to 5 priorities

- Repeat until you get to 2 to 3 priorities.

♦ Ask yourself Drucker's critical question: "What justifies you being on the payroll?" What is it that only a person in your role can do?

Those two or three main priorities should be the focus of your time. The other items are obviously important, but you need to find a way to delegate those items while ensuring that they get done. Drucker (2006) also notes that school executives and other not-for-profit leaders have an especially difficult time with this since everything appears to be a priority. This is due in part to the large number of goals we must focus upon and various constituents that we must please. He reminds us to focus our time upon those areas that will make the greatest contribution to the organization's goals.

Pareto Principle

The Pareto Principle is attributed to Italian economist Vilfredo Pareto. You may know his principle by the 80/20 rule. Pareto found that 80% of a company's sales were made by 20% of the company's sales force. The Pareto Principle was extended to describe various organizational issues that conform to this 80/20 rule; for example, 80% of your school's discipline problems come from 20% of your teachers. The Pareto Principle can be extended to your work as a busy school executive as well. Eighty percent of your success comes from twenty percent of your activities and time.

Once you have determined your top three priorities, block out the time on a daily or weekly basis to focus upon those three priorities. If you don't make the time on your calendar to spend time on your priorities, they simply will not get done or get done effectively. If there is no improvement in one of your top priorities, your superintendent will be certain to ask why. It would not be wise to say, "I just didn't want to do this priority." Instead, you might say, "I didn't have time to get this done." The superintendent's response will probably be, "Not good enough." Not finding the time to focus upon the most important priorities is generally indefensible.

When Actions Become A Project

A project is anything that takes more than a couple of action items to complete. You may be engaged in multiple projects at the same time. Some examples of projects include:

♦ A long standing committee upon which you serve

♦ Drafting, editing, and completing a report

♦ Compiling a summary of activities and results for a program review with your superintendent.

To keep your projects under control, find a way to keep them at the top of your mind. Three techniques (one low-tech and two electronic versions) can help you with this. The key with each of these strategies is to identify the action steps and due dates, and then monitor the results to ensure success.

Almost every school has an annual planning process that goes under the heading of school improvement plans or annual plans. Regardless of the title, every school has a plan on how to improve. Unfortunately, with many schools, the planning process goes awry when school improvement teams and school leaders don't think through or plan exactly what needs to be done by when. Let's take a simple example to illustrate project planning. You are working with your new teachers to plan a field trip. What has to happen for this field trip to go off flawlessly?

- Book the transportation

- Get field trip parent permission forms

- Determine how to pay for the field trip

- Get approval from the principal (and maybe Central Office)

- Ensure that there are learning activities before and after the field trip.

Once you have listed the major tasks that need to be completed, put them on one sheet of paper along with who is responsible for each of the activities, as shown in Figure 2.4.

FIGURE 2.4   Sample Project Plan

When	Who	What
1/24	John	Figure out how we are going to pay for the field trip
1/26	Sarah	Get approval from the principal (and maybe Central Office)
1/26	Sarah	Ensure that there are learning activities before and after the field trip
2/1	DeJuan	Book the transportation
2/4	Shanetta	Get field trip parent permission forms

After you have listed the major activities, place them in chronological order, assign a person to each activity, and then monitor the progress. One method for monitoring involves your 43 file folders that you had originally set up. You simply create a new file folder for the "field trip project," print out the task list along with all other information associated with this particular field trip (field trip forms, permission forms, itineraries, transportation information). This will be a good opportunity to use the 43 file folders we described earlier in this chapter. If your next action is due on the 26th, simply place the file in the hanging file folder labeled "26" and you can rest assured that you'll get to it on the 26th, rather than rely on your somewhat selective memory.

You can do the same thing by creating an untimed event on your electronic calendar or on your task list. On the subject line, underline the title of the project and on the location field insert the time that the project is due. You can then insert in the notes section of the appointment the dates and activities that have to be completed each day. You can simply copy and paste the information for the dates when different key results are due. As an added reminder, put the initials of the person responsible for that action step beside each one so you can easily remember with whom you need to talk.

Delegation

Few topics have been written about in greater detail than delegation. It is a critical task that separates an effective school executive from an individual contributor. Without delegation, your effectiveness is hamstrung. Three key elements in effective delegation are:

- deciding what to delegate

- the act of delegating

- tracking what you have delegated to others to ensure that the tasks and projects are completed on time and within the success parameters you have outlined.

Deciding What To Delegate

As a principal, you cannot do it all by yourself, so you must first decide what you can and should delegate. Some administrators suffer from the condition known as "perfectionism." To determine if you are among the afflicted, here is a simple two question test:

1. Can anybody do the job as well as you can do it? Yes or No.

This is actually a trick question. You were promoted to the principalship because you were a terrific individual contributor. Nobody can do all of these jobs as well as you can. After all, you have lots of experience and success in doing this job. Right? Well, now let's move to question number 2

2. Can anybody do this job, *period*?

This is also a trick question. Let's refer back to Drucker's question in the Pareto Principle, "What are the top two or three priorities that justify someone in your role being on the payroll?" You must take all of the other competing priorities and determine who else in your organization can and should do these tasks. Some of these assignments are obvious—they are part of another person's job description. Others are vague. You know the job must be done, but you are not sure who should do it. Part of your role as a school executive is to identify and develop talent. Note, there is a difference between developing and dumping. Some tasks and projects simply are a part of the work within the school. Be intentional about assigning stretch work or grunt work , and don't feel guilty about it.

Second, determine *how much* of a project or task to delegate. You can delegate some aspects of the task or delegate the entire task. William Oncken (1987) describes this as the difference between monkey management and managing gorillas. Monkeys, in his analogy, are individual tasks, while gorillas are an entire series of tasks or the entire project.

It might be helpful to think of the concept of "skill and will" as you decide how much of the project to delegate. Someone may have a great deal of enthusiasm for the task (high will) while not having any experience at all in doing the task (low skill). In a situation like this, it would be helpful to break down the tasks into individual pieces and monitor each closely, rather than give someone the entire project. Similarly, if a person has experience and skill in the task (high skill), but relatively little interest (low to medium will), it will be more productive to assign larger chunks without jeopardizing the entire project. We'll discuss monitoring below.

More Effective Delegating Strategies

Once you have decided *what* task or project you are delegating, think through *how* you will delegate this task or project to another person. Unfortunately, many of us have been in situations where we are told "Here's a project I want you to handle because you have been doing an outstanding job. Let me know when you've completed it." You are confused on what you are supposed to do, when you have to have it done, and how to complete the task.

The most effective delegation strategies have several keys in mind: *chunking, results, parameters, communication, and insurance policies.*

Chunking

Chunking involves thinking through how much of the job or task you can delegate to another person or team. You have several options as you decide what to delegate:

- ◆ You can break up the project into smaller pieces where the individual returns to you at a specified time and gives you an update,

- ◆ You can delegate the initial research or activities to another person after which you take over the second and third phase

- ◆ You can delegate the entire project to another person with periodic updates to you.

For example, you can use the sample list in Figure 2.5 with your administrative assistant by adjusting the assignment for her. Pick and choose from these items to start as a springboard for other items to delegate. You can create a similar list for other people that are your direct reports, such as your guidance counselor, department/grade level chairs, and assistant principal

Results and Parameters

Communicating your expectations for the task is critical. When talking with the person to whom you are delegating the task, you should be clear about the following:

- ◆ The expected result

- ◆ The task or project parameters. Parameters can include financial resources, due dates, and deliverables for milestones.

- ◆ Levels of authority include the types of independent decisions the individual can make solo and those decisions for which you need to provide guidance.

Figure 2.5 Delegation Ideas

Delegate	Beginner	Expert
Phones	Take messages and forward to appropriate person.	Filter calls, troubleshoot, initiate action and inform you on what they have done.
Mail	Open, sort into junk mail and important mail. Sort important mail into information items and action items. Type boilerplate/stock letters for your signature.	Toss junk mail, prepare drafts of action item mail and letters for your signature or edits. Highlight pertinent information items or summarize all information items in one word processing document.
Filing	Maintain current system, keep filing system up to date and current.	Design/streamline system. Periodically purge files for deletion.
Calendar	Confirm appointments day before. Arrange meeting logistics for internal and external meetings. Confirm attendees. Send out reminder agenda	Pull relevant files for the meetings. Assist on action items in 43 file folders. Block out time on principal calendar to do projects and key areas of responsibility.
Contact management	Enter new contacts.	Categorize contacts.
Reports and memos	Type as asked.	Generate first drafts of reports or complete reports and inform principal afterwards.
Supplies and equipment	Keep supplies in stock. Call and supervise repairs for office equipment.	Research supplier vendors to find ways to reduce costs.

♦ Due dates for individual checkpoints or milestones for the entire task or project.

♦ Performance measures. Performance measures may be quantitative or they may be requirements that must be completed.

This person's success will depend largely on your ability to communicate your expectations and how you will define success on this project.

Communication That Avoids Confusion and Time Loss

Remember the quiz on whether anybody can do the job better than you? Your role as an executive is to be very tight on *what* you want accomplished with the task, but allow individual freedom on *how* to complete the project within the parameters. The most effective executives clearly define the goal and outcome followed by the latitude to use creativity and judgment to accomplish the task. You want the individual to "own" the outcome, which tends to increase motivation for the result. Yet, if you know some parameters that will help the person avoid some potholes, be sure to share those thoughts.

Upward delegation occurs when the person you have delegated to comes to you with a problem and you promise to take the next step. Oncken (1987) has a wonderful analogy that illustrates upward delegation. He tells the story of monkeys (the next action or task) who jump from the assistant to the manager with great regularity. Oncken reminds us that effective managers don't let their subordinates push the next move onto them (allowing the monkey to jump off the subordinate's back to the manager's back). Imagine the subordinate requests a meeting with the manager to discuss his lack of progress due to unforeseen problems. The manager is there for consultation and support but the next move remains the responsibility of the subordinate, not the manager. In the rare occasion when the next move is yours, do your best to complete the next action step while the individual is with you to avoid confusion and time loss.

Delegation Insurance Policies

A delegation insurance policy is a way to ensure the person you have delegated to has not "vectored off into space." When you ask for updates and next actions, there are two possible actions the person can take (insurance policies).

1. They may ACT, then inform you after the fact.

2. They may RECOMMEND a course of action and proceed after you have given permission to do so.

Let's look at an example of how this might work with a team of four teachers who will be responsible for developing a schoolwide professional development plan for the upcoming year. As context, the faculty has engaged in analysis of the achievement test results for the past 2 years. Their analysis found consistently lower achievement results from children with mild to moderate special needs and children who speak English as a Second Language at a moderate level. In addition, children who are academically gifted have essentially flat-lined (have shown no growth) during the same period. The school leadership team has identified differentiating instruction within the regular classroom as a focus for professional development for the upcoming year. You've decided that you want to delegate the professional development plan to a team of two highly respected teachers and two teachers whom you want to develop into becoming strong team leaders. Your initial meeting with the team of four may sound something like this:

"We need your expertise to come up with a draft of the professional development plan for the upcoming school year. The focus of the plan should be improving achievement for students with special needs and English Language Learners (Results). It is also important that the entire faculty has a chance to provide input into the plan. We need to gain a better understanding of how to train and support teachers in differentiated instruction. In addition, be aware that some people may want to try different things. That's OK as long as their objectives and strategies fit within the established parameters (Parameters). Our schoolwide professional development budget is $1,000 for the entire year. It does not include trips to conferences and professional associations (Parameters). For the professional development plan to be a success, we need to ensure that all faculty have a chance to share ideas and key areas that they think will be important to look for in designing the professional development plan (Performance measures). The entire faculty will provide you with ideas and input but the final plan is up to the four of you (Levels of authority). Please come back Thursday afternoon with your ideas for how to most effectively get everybody's input along with any challenges or obstacles that you think we may run into (Due date, milestone, and deliverable). We need to have the professional development plan laid out and ready to go in 2 weeks and get any materials ordered, speakers or facilitators from either within the school or outside of the school—all completed in four weeks time (Deadline for entire project)."

Tracking and Monitoring Delegation Tasks and Projects

Now that you have delegated tasks or projects, your desk is clear and you can spend time in the classrooms. You are more confident that all of your tasks will be done on time, within the parameters and performance metrics. It's important for you to track and monitor delegated tasks with discipline and regularity. Tracking and monitoring delegated tasks demonstrates your commitment to the successful completion of the project. Tracking also helps you coach and mentor the people you have delegated to. Finally, tracking helps you develop your team's talent, to help them handle more challenging and even larger projects. Their increased expertise leverages your time to focus on your top three priorities.

Tracking Tasks

One tool to monitor the status of different projects is to have a tracking sheet for each person that you interact with frequently. This is part of the 43 file folders setup outlined earlier. Inside of each file folder, insert a copy of the task list in Figure 2.6.

Each time you meet with that person, pull out the tracking sheet and review where the person is on each of the tasks. If the task gets delayed for whatever reason, simply put the revised date on the sheet. This tracking sheet has the added advantage of giving you consistent and accurate information for performance reviews. One principal we know has a personal memo pad in a binder. As each meeting unfolds, this principal creates delegation tasks during the meeting, creating a running record for that person.

Figure 2.6   Task Tracker

Date Completed	Task/Person Responsible	Date Assigned	Due Date	Revised Date

You can use a similar model to monitor projects.

In the "who" column, record the person's initials who has the lead for that action step followed by the initials of people supporting that person. For instance, if you have a team of Pat Simpson (assistant principal), Helen Stokes (department chair), Dale Parker (principal), and Kelly Handley (guidance counselor) working on the master schedule and student scheduling for special needs students, the tasks might look like Figure 2.7.

FIGURE 2.7   Sample Task Tracker

Due	What	Who	Metric
3/1	Student course selections sent out	KH	Letter or e-mail
3/15	Student course selections returned	KH	All selections returned
4/1	Master schedule created for department	HS,PS	All class loads within district standards
6/15	Teachers interviewed and selected for department vacancies	DP,HS	Fully staffed by 7/1
7/20	Special needs student schedules run and checked for IEP compliance	KH, HS	All students course loads are in compliance with student IEPs

Monitoring Key Initiatives

You can use the same type of tracking system that we outlined above to monitor the key indicators of various initiatives. We'll give several examples to illustrate what some school executives have done to track different aspects of their school.

1. **Mentoring New Teachers:** New teachers have to be nurtured and supported during their first years in the profession. Every time a teacher leaves, you lose the time it takes for you to hire a new teacher in addition to the money you lost in providing staff development for that teacher who just walked out the door. One strategy is to set up frequent meetings between the new teacher and the mentor. One artifact you can use is to receive a one-paragraph summary of what the mentor and the new teacher discussed during their meetings. You can set up a monitoring system (one meeting once a week, for example) with a summary of discussion points. You want to balance the need for documentation with the demand on teacher's time for writing reports.

2. **Professional Development:** One frequent issue in the effectiveness of professional development is tracking the transfer of what was learned into the classroom. You can set up the metric on what you expect to see in the classroom based upon the school's staff development needs and subsequent professional/staff development. You can then measure what you want to see in the classroom based upon that metric. For example, your teachers returned from a conference excited about the idea of sharing unit plans based upon a common series of objectives that will

be taught during a 9-week period. Your metric can be tied to the teachers giving you a consistent unit plan with the objectives that will be taught each week. You can monitor by reviewing what they have given you with what you and your assistant principals see during the classroom walk-throughs.

3. **Technology in the Classroom:** The use of technology in the classroom can be monitored by looking at a checklist on how technology is being used during instruction. The school principal and assistant principals can take a quick look and talk quietly with the students who are on the computers to see if they are being used as free time, remediation, enrichment, or simply playing as a reward for completing their work. You can also check (if you want that level of specificity) to see whether all students have equitable access to computers.

4. **Classroom observations by assistant principals:** You can set a number of informal classroom observations by assistant principals each week. During weekly administrator team meetings, discuss what they have seen, trends they have found, what is going well, and what needs additional attention.

Your calendar is another tracking tool. For examples, as you are wrapping up a meeting, decide on the next steps and when you will meet for an update. You should log the appointment on your calendar (it is especially helpful when the person is watching you do this!) and agree to meet at a specific date and time. One highly effective school executive with a reputation for talent development uses this strategy with a twist. Three days before the person is supposed to meet with her, she speaks with the individual or e-mails the person a short message that says, "We're meeting in three days about XYZ. Do you need any information from me for this?" This comment helps remind the person that the principal is monitoring what she considers is important, thinks it is important enough to track and follow up, and is gently reminding the individual that there should be some movement and action on that item by the time they meet.

Parameters Save Precious Time

Two of your most precious resources are time and attention. You are accountable for the results of the work but you are not responsible for doing the work yourself. As you move into an executive role, you have to give your leadership team parameters on your expectations:

♦ When do you want them to engage you early in the project or issue to give additional perspective on the challenge?

♦ Under what circumstances do you want them to suggest two or three well thought-out options and the implications surrounding the options?

♦ Under what circumstances do you want them to come to you with the recommendation, the potential impact on various groups (positive and negative), and why they chose that particular recommendation?

For example, one principal had the opportunity to reduce class size in an elementary school. His school received funding for six additional full-time teacher assistant positions. This allotment had the flexibility to be used for the full-time teacher assistants (with benefits), part-time teachers (without benefits), or instructional supplies. This urban school was in a college town that had several stay-at-home former teachers who did not want to return to full-time work. The principal brought a carefully selected team together and laid out the parameters. He gave his perspective and insight on what the district board (and superintendent) had shared with him. He asked the team to:

- analyze the school's needs, based upon student achievement and state requirements

- analyze options for using the allotment

- return to him with options before the team goes into specific details about options and chooses an option.

The principal didn't want the team to go through a great deal of work and bring a recommendation without having some intermediate checkpoints. The team came back to him with their analysis of the school's biggest need: improved early intervention and achievement in the early grades for reading, mathematics, and writing. The committee also recommended reducing class size in the early grades by employing part-time teachers for 3 hours a day. The principal helped them think through several possible issues by asking questions like:

- Where would the part-time teachers be assigned to teach?

- How would students be assigned?

- What would be the financial impact? (for additional teacher editions, instructional supplies, for example)

- What would be the impact on reduced class size?

- How would they communicate this proposal to parents and teachers?

- What were the regulatory implications, such as building and fire codes, for this proposal?

- How would teachers be selected to share the same room? (noise level, instructional strategies, and noise tolerance)

His perspectives helped them think through the implications and unanswered questions. After much consideration, the school cut class size in half for first, second, third, fourth, and fifth grade classes for reading, math, and writing. Classrooms were divided by office cubicles, and baffles approved by the fire department were installed. The teachers focused on characteristics they wanted in their team teacher, such as whether they liked a lot of movement or not or whether they tolerated a lot of "instructional noise." The principal's contribution was asking questions and giving his perspective at critical moments.

Nobody has enough time, yet everybody has the same amount of time during the day and week. One trait that separates the exceptional school executives from the average administrator is how they leverage their time to focus upon their top priorities. The strategies discussed in this chapter will help you get the most out of your day and find more time for instructional leadership.

3
Data-Driven Decision Making

A principal lamented, "I keep hearing about how data should drive my decisions. My problem is that I'm drowning in data but I'm starved for information!" School executives frequently look for the "one thing" that will solve all of their problems. Leading your staff in making decisions based on facts and supported by data will have positive impact on student achievement and your school. The key is transforming data into information you can act on. This chapter will give you tools and frameworks to transform data into information for school improvement. Typical types of data used in school include:

+ gender

+ ethnic

+ age

+ socioeconomic status

+ teacher and student attendance

+ student achievement scores

The key for a school executive is to bring the facts to bear on the issue of school improvement. You might think of a mnemonic device, R^4, to remember the purpose of data-driven decision making (DDDM): The Right data to the Right people at the Right time to make the Right decisions.

+ **Right data**. You need to know the right data to bring to the table for the issues at hand.

+ **Right people**. You want to have the people at the table that can actually *do* something with the data and the subsequent action that will be required.

+ **Right time**. You need the data before you make decisions, not afterwards. Data gathered after the fact doesn't allow you to make corrections. It's like driving a car while looking through the rear-view mirror. You can tell where you've been, but it's hard to see where you are going.

♦ **Right decisions**. It is frequently noted that decisions should be made in the best interests of the children. Yet frequently, other agendas intrude upon the decision-making process. Using facts and information that is gained from the right type of data sources can help mitigate these other agendas.

School executives also need to focus less on statistics and look for richer sources of data that can give information for school improvement and growth. This relentless pursuit of facts to drive decisions can help focus resources that will be needed to implement your strategy.

Your team should also establish a baseline or benchmarks to track progress and guide midcourse adjustments. Before we describe our framework for data-driven decision making, we will discuss other sources of data that you should consider. These additional data points will help create a richer and more complete picture of the school's performance and provide context for the important decisions that follow.

Types of Data and Data Sources

Data sources can be grouped into four major areas: achievement, demographic, perception, and process data. People are generally familiar with the *student achievement* and *demographic indicators*. These two types of data are frequently used and misused by parents and the media to explain away or support various positions. Many states, as part of their reporting requirements, collect various types of demographic data, such as race, gender, socioeconomic status (for example, free and reduced lunch), special education categories, and parent education level in addition to student achievement data. Schools and districts now also may collect *perception data*, such as parent and teacher satisfaction surveys or other climate surveys. Finally, there are *data sources* that school executives have readily accessible but are not generally part of data-driven decision making. These data sources include staffing information (number of teachers with advanced degrees), scheduling information, financial information, and data collected in classroom observations. This wealth of data can lead you to think like the principal at the start of the chapter who is drowning in data but starving for information. One way to focus on transforming data into information is to think of "actionable data".

Actionable Data

Think through each set of data and ask, *"Can I do something with this?"*

This idea of actionable data helps you and your team focus on what you can improve, rather than engaging in fruitless discussions of topics that might be out of your reach. You likely haven't found an educator who was not concerned about the number of children born into poverty. Nor have you found an educator who had the financial and philanthropic resources to lift a community out of poverty single-handedly. Focusing upon areas that are within your control as educators can provide a much greater effect than those factors outside of your control. Perception and school process data are key tools in generating this effect. School process data is a "leading indicator" of school improvement and can be especially useful to the team.

Leading Indicators

A leading indicator is a term that assumes when one consistently acts in certain ways, then there is a good chance that something predictable will happen (If we do A, then B will happen more and more frequently). In education, we generally accept several ideas that are based in long-standing research in areas that we want to affect, such as those is Figure 3.1.

FIGURE 3.1 Leading Indicator Ideas

Doing "A"	will lead to	behavior "B"
Asking higher order questions	will lead to	improvement in the learner's ability to effectively and efficiently analyze, synthesize, and solve complex problems
Using higher student engagement strategies in classes	will	improve student achievement and reduce discipline problems
Using technology to help teach and extend the classroom	will	improve student engagement
Treating teachers with respect	will	increase teacher retention

A DDDM Framework

Data-driven decision making does not need to be difficult and depends largely on your ability to consistently apply the framework to different situations. The framework has three parts: analysis, strategy, and implementation.

Analyze: What are you trying to achieve? What facts are pertinent to the issue? What additional questions do you have?

This is where a systematic analysis can help. Determine what you want to accomplish and analyze the facts related to the issue. Create a fact pack, which is simply a listing of the strengths you find, the weaknesses you see, any questions you still have, and your information source. Your information sources may include district test score data for a certain year, retention data, and local school test data. When you create a fact pack, you are not looking at a doctoral dissertation or a lengthy discourse on educational research. This analysis should take you no more than a couple of hours to complete. Gather facts, focus the facts on the issue that you want to address, and create a plan to address the issue with timelines and accountability for results. We've created a fact pack template in Figure 3.2 on page 44.

Next, determine the actions steps, responsible people, timelines, and metrics for assessing progress. The source column gives you reference information in case you need to go back to confirm any data or if you are challenged by somebody on your data source. A sample template is shown in Figure 3.3 on page 45.

FIGURE 3.2   Fact Pack Template

Strengths	Weaknesses	Questions	Source

Strategy: What will you do to accomplish your goal?

Strategy is covered extensively in the chapter, "How to Ensure Your School Improvement Plan Works." The performance metrics may be difficult to nail down in the beginning, but you should put time into determining how you will know whether the action has been accomplished. If you skip this step, it will be impossible to determine if the responsible person has completed the assignment. And equally important to ask is, Was the intended result due to this strategy or some other intervening factors?

Implementation: What items and assignments need to be monitored?

The form above outlines one way to track what actually gets done. Managing the project on one page eliminates scraps of paper and documents all over your desk. You can put this document and any supporting documentation in a file folder to keep it all in one place. We recommend inserting the tracking form in one of your 43 file folders explained in chapter 2, "Finding Time for Instructional Leadership."

That is where Analysis, Strategy, and Implementation tie together with a data-driven decision making model. Let's take a look at two examples where you can translate data into information and use the facts as a basis for change.

Example #1: Classroom Technology Usage

You have invested significant time and money into creating technology access for your students. Almost every school these days has a fully functioning computer lab. Now might be a good time to analyze how effectively the technology is being used by your teachers and students in the classroom. You might analyze this with the following framework:

What do you want to accomplish?

Goal: Improved student achievement for all students

FIGURE 3.3 Action Planner Template

What do we want to accomplish? _____

Observations/ facts	Questions that still need answers	Strengths	Areas needing improvement	Source

Recommendation:

Result (should be almost identical to what you want to accomplish)	End Date

Timeline

Date	Who	What	Performance Measure

FIGURE 3.4   Leading Indicator Sample-Classroom Technology

Doing "A"	will lead to	behavior "B"
Using technology to differentiate instruction for struggling and talented students	will lead to	Improved student achievement for struggling students as well as students who are academically talented

Assumptions:

Using our model (see Figure 3.4) from the leading indicators section on data-driven decision making, we make the following assumptions:

a. Technology can facilitate differentiated instruction for students needing remediation and acceleration. All students benefit from using technology.

b. Using technology can help increase student achievement.

How will you analyze classroom technology usage?

During classroom observations or informal classroom visits, look for evidence of how technology is being used by students and teachers. If you have assistant principals, you can and should enlist their help in collecting the data. You'll do this in two phases to answer the question: *"Are the computers turned on and being used by any students?"*

PHASE I: First, go to your tech support person and have the tech support certify that all computers are working and operational. Next, collect data on how many computers are turned on and being used (see Figure 3.5). Depending on the number of classrooms, we suggest that you divide the building and assign rooms for data collection to prevent duplication of efforts or missed classrooms.

Then you summarize the data to answer questions like

1. Do you have operational computers in all of the classrooms? Is that important? (You are testing your assumptions).

2. Do you have any teachers who consistently use computers? Are there any teachers who consistently have the computers turned off? Is that important?

FIGURE 3.5   Computer Utilization – Data Collection Form #1

Monday   Tuesday   Wednesday   Thursday   Friday   (circle one)

Teacher	# of Computers	# of Computers Turned On	# of Computers Used

FIGURE 3.6   Computer Utilization – Data Collection Form #2

Teacher	Date	Grade (or Department)	How Used (I-instructional, E-early completion, G-games, N-not used, U-unable to determine)

PHASE II: You've collected some important data in your first week. Assuming that you think that using computers is important to student success, your second phase of data collection might focus on whether the computers are being used for instructional purposes, as rewards for early completion of work, or for games. You can create a similar table, Figure 3.6 to your first data table to gather this data in the second week. Increasingly, school executives require that teachers post on the whiteboard/chalkboard the day's instructional objective. You can quickly glance at the instructional objective and then cross-reference the stated objective with your observation of what is going on with the computers. This can help you gauge how computers are being used at your school.

Two quick notes:

1. You can certainly do this type of data collection on a spreadsheet that you have on a mobile PC, on a smart phone, or with clipboard and paper. You can then transfer the data to a spreadsheet to see patterns more easily by using the Sort, Filter, and pivot table commands.

2. You need enough good data to analyze and make decisions. Simply getting one or two observation data points is not enough to make good decisions. In this example, you have two weeks of data to ensure that there is a representative sample across grade levels/departments, by teacher, and by time of day.

You can then start to analyze patterns to see how the computers are being used. This data can have a big impact on your school's professional development, individual teacher growth plans, focus of informal observations, and resource allocation, and it provides a topic for grade level/departmental professional learning communities.

Example #2: Student Discipline Referrals

Student discipline is a perennial issue for many school executives. You can use a similar DDDM framework to decrease student discipline and increase the amount of time the students have in the classroom to learn the material.

What do you want to accomplish?

Goal: Decreased student discipline referrals resulting in in-school or out-of-school suspension

Assumptions:

  a. Analyzing patterns in discipline referrals can help identify positive steps to reduce disruptions to the learning environment and increase the amount of time students are present in the classroom.

  b. Increased time in class will result in increased student achievement.

How will you analyze discipline data?

Almost every discipline referral form has the following data points: name, race, gender, teacher, offense, and action taken. Simply adding three other fields in a database or spreadsheet application (day of week, time of day, and location) can help find patterns to help reduce discipline referrals and increase the amount of time available for instruction. Two quick examples can illustrate how you might use this data to suggest interventions and solutions to help address the issues.

EXAMPLE 1

A high school found that over 40% of discipline referrals occurred on Monday and Friday mornings in the bus parking lot and cafeteria. When the principal "ran the data", she found that her students appeared to engage in "home issues" that were carried to school on Mondays and Fridays. The principal was surprised by the high number of referrals on those 2 days. The principal brought the data to her school leadership team. The school leadership team decided to increase the number of professional staff in those two areas on Monday and Friday mornings only; then return to their normal staffing patterns for the other days of the week. After an initial upsurge in discipline referrals (where admittedly they were worried that their plan was not working), they saw almost a 30% drop in discipline referrals, which led to more time for the students to learn in the classroom.

EXAMPLE 2

An elementary school assistant principal found that a large majority of the discipline referrals came from a small group of teachers with the discipline offense of "disrespect." The assistant principal took a four-prong approach to resolve the problem:

  1. The assistant principal talked with teachers to determine what behaviors defined "disrespect."

  2. The assistant principal worked with the guidance counselor to create lessons and modules on appropriate behavior.

  3. The assistant principal then looked at factors the school had identified as important to decreasing discipline referrals. The assistant principal found that more effective teachers used dramatically different instructional strategies than less effective teachers (see Figure 3.7).

  4. The assistant principal worked with those teachers with lower student engagement rates to find different instructional practices to increase their student engagement rates.

After 2 months, the discipline referrals related to disrespect went down by 40%.

FIGURE 3.7 Discipline Referrals Sample Log

Teacher	Observation Date	Student Engagement (H, M, L)	Student Work	Teacher Work	Type Work
Jones	5-Sep	H	C	C	HO
Oaker	6-Sep	L	W	LL	L
Meedy	7-Sep	L	I	L	W
Jones	16-Sep	H	P	C	HO
Oaker	16-Sep	L	W	L	L
Meedy	17-Sep	L	W	W	DP
Jones	23-Sep	H	I	C	T
Meedy	23-Sep	M	W	W	DP
Jones	4-Oct	M	W	W	DP
Meedy	5-Oct	L	I	L	DP
Oaker	6-Oct	M	W	L	L
Jones	14-Oct	H	C	W	HO
Meedy	15-oct	L	I	C	W
Oaker	18-Oct	M	I	L	L
Jones	26-Oct	H	P	C	HO
Oaker	29-Oct	L	I	W	L
Meedy	30-Oct	L	W	W	HO
Jones	7-Nov	H	I	W	T
Meedy	9-Nov	M	W	W	W
Oaker	11-Nov	H	W	L	DP
Jones	16-Nov	M	C	C	DP
Oaker	17-Nov	L	I	L	L
Meedy	18-Nov	L	W	L	HO
Jones	3-Dec	H	P	C	W
Meedy	5-Dec	L	W	C	W
Oaker	6-Dec	M	W	L	L
Oaker	9-Dec	M	I	W	DP
Oaker	11-Dec	L	W	L	DP
Meedy	11-Dec	M	W	L	DP

In this example, the **Student Engagement** column had High (more than 85% of the students engaged); Medium (75–84% engaged); and Low (less than 85% engaged). The **Student Work** column shows Centers/cooperative groups (C); Pairs/triads (P); Independent (I); and Whole class (W). The **Teacher Work** column shows Lecture (L); Coaching (C); and Whole class (W). The **Type Work** column indicates Worksheet or questions in book (W); Drill and practice (DP), Technology (T), Higher Order thinking skills (HO), and Listening to teacher (L).

4
Resource Management

Many school executives are extremely uncomfortable talking about the school's budget, the various resources available, and how school executives can use the school budget as an effective instructional leadership tool. When asked, their discomfort ranges over the following:

- an inordinate fear of over or under committing the money

- getting in trouble with the legal system

- losing their job

- being embarrassed by their colleagues, faculty, and community members.

This chapter will demystify the topic of school finance and show how to use the budgeting process as a key driver for reaching your school's goals.

Myths of Effective Resource Management

There are some myths surrounding school budgeting and finance.

Myth: I should have a math, accounting, or a business background to be able to effectively build and run a budget.

Reality: There is absolutely no reason that a school leader cannot learn to develop, implement, and monitor a budget. Budgeting doesn't require sophisticated mathematical knowledge or any business skills. The only mathematical skills you need are the four arithmetic operations: addition, subtraction, multiplication, and division. What is critical is discipline, drive, and focus; skills that are available for almost every school executive.

Myth: Curriculum and instruction is supposed to be my focus; budgeting should be handled by someone else. I didn't sign up to be a school leader to write checks and monitor the balance on the budget. My focus has to be on the students in my school.

Reality: The school leader's role has changed dramatically in the past 15 years. School leaders are now seen as either small CEOs (in terms of funds available to them) or vital middle managers who are crucial to the school and school system's success. School leaders also have the entire spectrum of instructional leadership as their core mission in addition to human resources (HR) management, operations, transportation, food service, and community relations. Nobody denies that being able to do all of these skills effectively is difficult. Yet, being an effective financial manager can help you steer additional resources to your most pressing needs—either with an instructional program, a targeted group of students, or both. In fact, school budgeting and resource management is an essential tool to implement your instructional vision. Initiatives without resources remain as a hope, not a reality. Moreover, effective school leaders are adept at reallocating resources to support instructional changes.

Myth: Budgeting is too hard and takes too much time.

Reality: There has been a significant shift in the amount of time required to develop and monitor a school budget. Budget development typically takes the biggest investment of time due to the need to align school goals with future resources and involve others in the process. Building a school budget will be discussed later in this chapter. Yet, once the budget is set, it generally takes less than 5 hours a month to monitor the budget. The exception to the 5 hours a month occurs if you see a variance between what you have budgeted and what you see expensed on your budget printouts.

Myth: I can't do anything about my budget anyway. It is given to me from central office and I have no control over it.

Reality: When school leaders demonstrate they have more than a passing knowledge of how the monies are distributed and how they can be spent, central office executives gain more confidence in their financial acumen and become more open to their involvement. More and more central office executives are excited about getting a chance to work with school-based leaders who know how to leverage greater gains from dollars allocated to them. This frequently results in increased flexibility for these informed school-based leaders.

Myth: The budget is nothing more than a checkbook. I just have to make sure I am not overdrawn at the end of the year.

Reality: Take your checkbook analogy as an example. You take money out from the monthly paycheck to pay for the mortgage or rent, groceries, insurance, utilities, and to pay off other loans. Money left over is your discretionary money to spend on your personal priorities. Your priorities may be a house, a new car, a vacation, or your child's education. The same prioritization holds true with school finance. You allocate money to the most important priorities for you and your school first and then work backward to pay for other priorities.

Myth: I don't have time to do this. My bookkeeper should be the one handling the money. She should just tell the teachers and me when we are running low on funds for copy paper.

Reality: Your school secretary or school-based bookkeeper should know more than you do about the different budget codes and what restrictions are placed upon each individual line item in the budget. That knowledge is a critical piece of her job. Yet, the bookkeeper cannot and should not be the one deciding **how** the funds should be spent. Aside from the gross negligence on your part, you open yourself up to charges of incompetence and inadequate internal controls that invite the possibility of fraud.

Myth: I never got any training in how to budget. I didn't get any practical help on how to budget either from my college courses or on the job. I can't even balance my own checkbook.

Reality: Few people have natural talent or extensive training to be a skilled budgeter. University preparation programs cannot hope to give you all the knowledge you need to become a successful school leader. Many school leaders end up learning school budgeting from their principal or mentor. This knowledge, which is akin to the grand oral tradition of passing along values by storytelling, is constrained by the skill of the storyteller and the stability of the knowledge. As we discussed earlier, school leadership has changed dramatically in the past 15 years. The adage "you never stop learning" is quite applicable here as well.

How Money Gets to Your School

There are four keys to getting the most out of your financial resources. You must know the funding source, the amount, the purpose, and the timeframe for spending the money. When you know these four points, paradoxically, you have more freedom to get the most out of those resources.

Fund Sources

Each school receives funds from one or more of these sources: state appropriations, local appropriations, federal appropriations, grants, and receipts from different activities (athletic, band, clubs, etc.). Each of these funding sources comes with a different timeline for action, cycles, and restrictions. The two biggest sources of funds are state and local appropriations. These two types of appropriations will vary in the percentage that come to the school and school district, but they are allocated to your school in a similar fashion.

Federal, state, and local governments operate on a 12-month fiscal year. The fiscal year may or may not be aligned with the January–December calendar year. At the state and local levels, the budget process starts almost a year in advance. Generally, about 9 months before the start of the new fiscal year, the superintendent and local school board begin their budget preparation for the upcoming year. They prepare the budget request to go to their local school board. Sometimes these meetings go smoothly; at other times, these meetings can be fairly contentious. As you hear about these budget deliberations, remember that:

♦ Funding is a key indicator of the different priorities of each group.

♦ The groups of people who approve the budget and allocate funds to the school district and to the school often have multiple and competing interests for the same dollars.

♦ State and local leaders generally have these three competing interests for revenue: education, medical assistance for the indigent and elderly, and public safety. Some call this "education, medication, and incarceration."

These three areas generally get the lion's share of the local and state funds.

Grants

Grants are an important source of additional funds. Grants are tied to improvement in specific areas, to target a specific group of students, or to implement a certain program or initiative. A common grant structure provides start-up funds to implement the initiative. Generally, grant funders expect ongoing funds at the school or district level will be used to take over the grant's impact when the grant runs out. Grants are frequently categorical funds and must be spent on only what was specified in the grant. When you go to a new school, be sure to see if you are obligated to any course of action based upon any grant funding.

Federal Funding

Federal funds are sent to schools based upon the federal government's desire to improve education from a policy perspective. United States senators and representatives are faced with multiple and competing interests for our tax dollars. While the percentage of school funds that come from the federal government is pretty low, generally less than 20%, those funds carry a great deal of clout. We only have to look at funding based upon No Child Left Behind (NCLB), vocational education, child nutrition, and special education to see how influential these federal dollars can be.

State and Local Funding

Constitutionally, public education is a state function. States and local governments provide the vast majority of funding for the school buildings, salaries, nutrition, transportation, and instructional supplies. As such, state and localities provide the backbone for educational funding. Different states and localities have different funding formulas. Some states have a heavy emphasis upon state funding. Others have a more localized approach, with localities having taxing authority.

Ancillary Funding

Another source of funds come from any sort of ancillary or extracurricular activities. Most of the time, these activities come from the high school level. Two examples that fall under this category are onsite child care centers and vocational education spin-offs like auto repair and construction.

School Level Funds

Finally, almost all schools have individual school accounts. Individual school accounts are like a checkbook in that there are few (if any) categorical requirements for these funds, other than restrictions that are informally in place. Fund-raisers, soft drink sales, snack sales, picture sales, and other forms of revenue generation all fall into the individual school accounts. In most schools, PTA, PTO , PTSO, and booster clubs for various activities (athletics, arts, drama, and band) are handled by that group's governing board. While you may not control these finances, you can and should influence the discussion to distribute the funds to improve the school. You should be prepared to provide guidance on how these funds should be spent based on the school's priorities.

Allotments

Funds generally flow to the school based upon an allotment formula. Allotments can be created based upon students, teachers, or different subgroups. The school has a certain number of students who are in the pool for a certain funding category. The budget officer then has a number of dollars, based upon the final budget allocated to the school district, that follow a particular child. Those funds are allotted to the school based upon the number of students that are in that particular category. Students who fit in multiple categories are counted multiple times. Let's take a simple example to illustrate the allotment process.

Coastalmont School has 500 students. Coastalmont's student population also has the following categories:

- ♦ 40 students receiving special education services

- ♦ 100 students who qualify for free lunch

- ♦ 75 students who qualify for reduced lunch

Coastalmont's district has a policy of having a class size of no more than 25 children in a classroom (a 1:25 classroom ratio).

The district also allocates $75/child receiving instructional resources, $40/child who is receiving special education services, $50/child who receives free lunch, and $35/child who receives reduced lunch.

Coastalmont's allotments are:

- ♦ 25 classroom teachers (500 students divided by the 1:25 ratio)

- ♦ $37,500 for instructional resources ($75 multiplied by the 500 students)

- ♦ $1,600 for special education services ($40 multiplied by the 40 students identified with special needs)

- ♦ $50,000 for children on free lunch ($50 multiplied by the 100 students receiving free lunch)

- ♦ $2,625 for children on reduced lunch ($35 multiplied by the 75 students receiving reduced lunch).

Allotments may have some restrictions attached to them. For example, funds for special education may be used only for students receiving those services. Allotments may come in three major forms: dollar allotments, categorical allotments, or position allotments. The fictional Coastalmont school has examples of all three types of allotments.

- *Dollar allotments* are very similar to a checkbook. The school gets a certain dollar amount, based upon a a predetermined allotment formula. The numbers are plugged into the formula and the total amount is given to the school. The school must live within the means of the dollar allotments.

- *Categorical allotments* are funds that are given to the school to help a particular group (category) of students. Generally, categorical allotments may be used ONLY for students who have that categorical designation are being funded. Special education and Title I are two of the best known and most common types of categorical allotments. Special education funds may be used only for children receiving special education services. Title I funds may only be used for children who are below the federal poverty level.

- Career Education funds must also be spent to support vocational programs, career counseling, and the equipment and supplies called for in the curriculum for these areas. Principals must also be careful not to assign classes or duties during the school day that are outside of the job responsibilities mandated by the funding source. Examples of inappropriate assignments might be study hall, SAT prep, and an entire period of lunch duty that is longer than other teachers are required to fulfill.

- *Position allotments* are funds that are spent on different positions within the school—teachers, teacher assistants, secretarial staff, principal and assistant principal salaries, and other salaried positions within the school.

When you are promoted or transferred to a new school, you should quickly schedule a meeting with your school district's financial officer to determine if there are restrictions and what flexibility you have in spending the funds at your assignment. Your district level financial officer may be able to help you gain additional flexibility, but she can only do this if you involve her early on in your deliberations. Finance officers and your immediate supervisor do not like surprises, especially if it involves the taxpayers' money.

You may hear the term "commingling of funds." Commingling is where two different funds are joined together and brought into one account. Usually, commingling is bad, because it makes it more difficult to keep track of the money where taxpayer money is being used.

Uniform Chart of Accounts

School districts follow a series of rules governing and tracking different types of funds. These rules are codified in a system called the Uniform Chart of Accounts (UCA). The UCA is used to identify the funding source and the purpose of each line item in the school-level budget. It is useful for you to obtain a copy of your school system's or state's UCA to learn the degree of flexibility each fund and code allows.

You may see your district's UCA as a series of numbers and letters similar to the example below:

A-BBB-CCC-DDD

Frequently, the UCA starts with a series of numbers or letters that serves as a large filter. Each succeeding series of letters and/or numbers further define and filter the funds in greater detail. Usually, the UCA starts with the four funding sources we discussed at the start of the chapter: the state allotments, local allotments, federal allotments, and grants. Those are usually the first digits. The next series of numbers generally indicate for which "buckets" the funds are intended, such as regular education, special education, child nutrition, transportation, or community services. The third set of digits further filters the funds into whether the funds will go to classroom teachers, children with special needs, staff development, technology, vocational education, remediation for children placed at-risk, or transportation. Finally, there may be another set of digits that outline exactly what the funds are used for: instructional supplies, workshop expenses, library books, computers, software, teacher salary, field trips, or even substitute payroll.

Building Your Budget

Now that you know the funding source, timeframe, purpose, and amount of your allotments, you can begin to build your annual budget. While you may want to see what was allocated in different categories in years past, you'll improve your school's chances for success by following these tactics in building your budget.

Creating a Fact Base

Your school has an abundance of statistics that are key parts of a fact base. Your fact base may include data such as the following:

- number of students
- number and percentage of children who are achieving on below grade level, on grade level, or above grade level
- teacher credentials
- student and teacher attendance data
- demographic information
- climate survey information

By creating a fact base, you can use the facts as a foundation upon which to base most decisions within the school. Schools budgets should be aligned with the stated mission adopted by the faculty and supported by current multiple sources of data such as student performance, parent and staff surveys, and student demographics. Business organizations refer to this process as "creating a fact base." This will necessarily create a dynamic tension between the need to sustain traditional programs and your attempts to allocate resources to help improve your school. Your fact base can go a long way to helping you make difficult choices in resource allocation.

Without facts, you are significantly hampered in your decision-making. You also run the risk of having a noisy minority opinion that can speak loudly to another agenda. A well developed fact base can give you confidence when responding to someone trying to push through a pet project by saying, "That's not what I understand the facts to be. In fact, here's what I have as the facts. What facts do you have to support your suggestion or recommendation?" Creating your fact base for the current year will take you between 10–20 hours. Allocate this time up front. It will pay huge dividends for you for the upcoming year. Remember that resources in this context include people, time, facilities, and money.

- ♦ Your fact base should be 3 or 4 pages maximum. Otherwise, you begin to run the risk having more detail than you need.

- ♦ Your fact base should take into account the most important factors that help drive your school forward or serve as an anchor for the school.

- ♦ Your fact base should, as much as possible, be actionable. Actionable means that the data is something that you can do something about or influence. You may have a keen interest in the number of green-eyed, left-handed students in your school, but if there is nothing that you can take action on, it is irrelevant to your fact base.

- ♦ You should include multiple sources of data for your fact base. Focusing solely upon student achievement and your budget will be insufficient. At a minimum, you should look at your student achievement, your student, teacher, and community demographics, and your available resources.

For a more detailed look at creating a fact base, check chapter 3 "Data Driven Decision-Making" in this book.

Equipment Replacement Cycles

Another part of a comprehensive fact base is an analysis of your equipment replacement cycles. Audio/visual equipment, textbooks, copiers, science equipment, vocational education equipment, library books, band equipment, athletic equipment, computers, printers, and related equipment are the most common groups of equipment that you need to review for periodic replacement. If you learn that your science equipment hasn't been replaced in over a decade and you are getting ready to implement a new hands-on science program, that information certainly needs to enter into your budgeting process. You can check with your central office, a regional service center, or your department of education to get additional information on what general replacement cycles are commonly used as benchmarks for replacement.

Historical Information

A third area that is useful for you in developing your fact base is to look historically at what has been spent in different categories. Find your end-of-year budget printouts for the previous 3 years, or access your budget online. End-of-year expenses can and should tell you the biggest expenses in each specific category. Examine your instructional supply and equipment line items closely. You can highlight or mark the vendors or items that seem to come up frequently. You should take a look not only at the frequency but also at the amount of your large expenditures. If you have online access, sort the data by the amount spent and look at your top spending vendors or items. You may think that your copier expense is excessive, yet you may be shocked at the excess when you actually run the numbers to determine the amount and proportion of money that is spent on copiers and duplicating equipment and supplies.

Working With Stakeholders

Once a fact base has been created, share it with the school's stakeholders. Consider who to share this information with and in what order. First, share this information with your supervisors and ask their advice on how to proceed. Next you should inform the leadership or school improvement team. The last group would be the Parent Teacher Association and other community groups. Faculty members, because of their focus and role, initially may not know what trends or issues are cropping up at the school level. They may not know how the trends they see (or don't see) in their grade or department level impact the entire school. Your internal leadership team is invaluable in helping you to determine trends and implications of the facts shared. Your manager or supervisor needs this fact base to help see what district resources might be reallocated to your school. This is especially true if your facts are outside the district priorities. Many schools now have formal school leadership teams or school improvement teams, made up of teachers, parents, and community members. Community groups and service organizations are generally willing to help once they see the need and understand your strategy to try to meet your goals. After sharing the fact base, goals, and strategies for meeting these goals with your stakeholders, you may well find that these outside groups can help provide resources (money, time, people, and space) to help you accelerate your completion of these goals.

Creating the fact base is the first step in developing your strategy for achieving the school's goals. A critical next step is determining your school's priorities and goals. In some cases, the goals are set for you. At this writing, the federal NCLB legislation provides a framework for goals that must be attained, along with state and district goals as well. Use your fact base and your budget to help achieve these goals. Chapter 8, "How to Ensure Your School Improvement Plan Works," provides greater detail on how to align resources with strategy.

Key Reasons to Monitor Your Budget

It will be tempting to breathe a sigh of relief when you have determined how allocated monies are going to be spent. However, if you fail to monitor how expenses are tracking against your plan, you will run into significant difficulties when unexpected issues arrive. Monitoring the budget will help you deal with the unexpected, but it is also a tactical necessity for getting additional resources each spring.

Dealing With Unexpected Issues

You should anticipate unexpected changes in priorities as the year progresses. For example, the staff may have requested additional resources to support hands-on instruction in the science curriculum. After budgeting to purchase materials for inquiry-based learning, you are made aware of a significant drop in students' reading scores. You then have a choice: You can either continue with your previous plan, or you can adjust or reallocate resources to meet the challenge of reading. Whatever your decision, it needs to come from a reasoned (yet rapid) analysis of the data and the assumptions behind the decisions you made.

You will likely have additional challenges that will demand attention. Some examples include fluctuating prices for items such as maintenance of computers and printers, copiers and paper, instructional, instructional supplies, or fuel for transportation/buses throughout the year. In many cases, your finance or purchasing departments will give you an alert before you place the order. Principals need to monitor their expenditures to avoid having a purchase order returned after several weeks due to insufficient funds. Most finance systems allow the budget manager (principal) to transfer undesignated funds from one account to another provided there is a sound reason.

Another prudent practice to combat fluctuations or budget shortfalls is to set aside between 15% to 20% of funds as an emergency reserve at the start of the year. This also allows you to also have a "war chest" to keep previously identified priorities at the forefront in volatile circumstances. Set aside that money until the end of the third month of school, spend half of it, and then repeat the process by the end of the seventh month. Another strategy is to ask your central office purchasing or finance department if you can add another single-digit number to purchase orders coming from your school that tie to your priorities in your school's uniform chart of accounts. This number would be the same year after year, but you would note internally whether you are indeed allocating the financial resources that you said you were going to use to help move your school forward.

A note of caution: In uncertain financial times, do not wait too long to spend your funds. When faced with a budget shortfall, state or local governments are often forced to freeze purchasing or retract unspent funds. By looking at purchase orders from the previous school year, you can project what you will need to meet the needs of your staff for the remainder of the school year.

End-of-Year Tactics

Many successful school executives use a strategy each spring to get additional resources for their school. Other school executives marvel at how, somehow, these successful principals get those additional monies to help their students. You can maximize your chances to get additional funds at the end of the year by following the tactics below.

Spend your allocated monies, know where you have spent your funds, and ensure that your funds are spent on your school or district priorities. Before you can ask for any additional funds, you need to know where your monies are currently being spent and on what initiatives. The people controlling the purse strings of the district want to know the answers to three simple questions:

♦ *Are you spending your school funds on your school or district goals?* If you are asking for more money, you had better ensure that your current resources are being spent upon initiatives that have been approved and implemented. You must demonstrate that you are spending your resources upon the initiatives that have previously been approved.

♦ *Do you know where your funds are being spent?* Once you request additional funds, your manager will ask the finance department for some basic research. The superintendent will want to know and will undoubtedly cross-check to ensure that you are spending funds on previously agreed-upon goals and initiatives. If the numbers do not match your story, you will lose significant (if not complete) credibility with your superiors, and future requests will be scrutinized even more carefully.

♦ *Have you already spent your school funds on these priorities as well as the regular running of the school?* The superintendent may want to know if you have "some skin in the game" investment in your request, rather than simply asking for more money for some pet project. In other words, have you allocated funds at your disposal before asking for additional monies?

Spend or encumber your funds by the end of the seventh month of your fiscal year. One of the most hated words to a school finance officers' ears is "reversion." Reversion occurs when the school or district has to return unused money to the funding source (local, state, or federal governments). Reversion also indicates to the funding authorities that "You didn't spend what you got this year. You obviously didn't need that money. We will reduce the funding to you by that amount for the following year." Reversion embarrasses finance departments and senior executive management. Many finance departments employ budget cycles to avoid reversion. During the first phase of the cycle, budget managers should spend about 60% of their funds by the 4th month of your school year. If you are in a traditional calendar school, you should have over half of your money spent by the end of the 6th month. At the mid-point in the school year, budget managers should begin to encumber or obligate their funds for anticipated purchases for the remainder of the school year. Most finance departments analyze each school and division's spending and encumbrances against each school's and division's budgeted amounts. Any variances between the two (under or over budget) are then analyzed which may result in a leftover sum of money. The superintendent and finance officer do not want to revert this money, so they look at what initiatives or projects they can inject with a one-time infusion of funds that will have the greatest impact.

Unlike the commercial sector, almost all school systems work under the model that "this year's funds are for this year's students." If you don't spend all of your allocated funds during one fiscal year, you cannot "roll it over" or bank the funds for the following year. The funds entrusted to your stewardship are to be used for the benefit of this year's students. This tenet provides you the opening to get additional funding by following the rest of the steps outlined here.

Determine your success on particular projects/programs/initiatives based upon previously determined metrics. Before you ask for funds, you should demonstrate that your current investments in current funds and expenditures are helping students succeed. You must have performance measures, baseline information, and current results. You stand a much lower chance of getting your requested additional one-time funding if you cannot demonstrate results. Like you, your manager, finance officer, and superintendent are all under pressure to demonstrate results. They want to be able to continue to move the school district forward. Your charge is to align your request for additional one-time funding with those priorities of the district and clearly show how you have been a good steward of your school's funds and how they have made helped students succeed. Generally, you have to write a short case to demonstrate your need and how the funds will be spent. Even if it is not required, your short brief will move your request higher in that pile of requests from different schools and departments.

Create a short case for additional resources, breaking down one-time expenses and continuing expenses. You should create a short two- or three-page (maximum) case outlining your request. Your case should include the following:

- a one page executive summary (with lots of white space)

- a one- or two-page narrative outlining the goal/initiative

- your results to date

- how you have spent your allocated funds to achieve the results

- your additional spending request

- a summary breakdown of how the money will be spent

These steps may streamline your proposal/case:

Start with page 2. Resist the impulse to write the summary first. Start with what you have achieved so far with your allocated funds, show your results, and how you want to spend any additional funds you might receive.

Write your executive summary. Effective written communication is tailored for the audience. Your audience (your superintendent, your manager, and your finance officer) are all very busy people. They want the summary in bullet form with lots of white space around the summary for their notes. You have the detail behind the summary *if* they want the background information. Think of your proposal as a pyramid. Your summary is at the top, and the supporting detail is underneath it. Your readers will read the proposal from top to bottom. Avoid writing your proposal like a mystery novelist who keeps the reader in suspense until the last page or scene. We've listed an executive summary sample below:

Request for $12,000 for 6 additional laptops for computer lab

We are requesting $12,000 for six additional laptop computers for Coastalmont School to allow for a full classroom set for students mainstreamed into the regular classroom. This $12,000 would supplement the existing $70,000 we invested this year for two mobile computer labs.

Background:

♦ Additional students enrolled after the funding cutoff, increasing class size by 1–2 students per classroom.

♦ Reallocated class rosters to provide for additional opportunities for main-streaming by students with special needs (District Priority #2-Success for All Students), increasing class size by 1–2 students.

♦ Invested $70,000 of Title I funds this year from school allotment for two mobile computer labs to integrate technology into the classroom (District Priority #5-Technology Equity of Access) through our local School Improvement Leadership Team.

♦ This would be a one-time funding, we would handle the ongoing mainte-nance of computers.

♦ Funding, if approved, would be used to purchase three additional comput-ers for each of the two mobile computer labs.

Keep both the district finance officer and superintendent informed, then ask for addi-tional funds at a strategic time. When asking for more money, timing is critical. Draft your case by the end of the 5th month of the school year, double check your figures and results at the 6th month, and ask for an appointment with the finance officers and superintendent at the end of the 6th month. This sequence is important. During months 1–4 of the school year, you are monitoring the funds entrusted to you. Everybody wants more money for their programs. You want to ensure that you can say you have spent your currently allocated funds . At the 5th month, most district finance officers have a pretty good idea of what funds have already been allocated and what funds have the chance of being swept into a central account.

One approach might be to ask questions at the initial meeting without making a formal request for additional funds. Instead, you ask some questions about the current budget and whether there is any chance for funding any one-time monies for the district's priorities. Confirm the district priorities since they may have been modified somewhat during the year due to unexpected circumstances. While you are "interviewing" them, you want to plant the seeds that you are doing some great things that tie to those district priorities. During the last 2 minutes of your 10-minute conversation, you ask if you might put together a proposal that you think has potential to reach and help even *more* of the students that are involved in the initiative. Ask them what information they would want or need to ensure that they could make a reasoned decision. Also ask them *when* they would need the information. You are now armed with additional information to quickly modify and revise your proposal to hit the current hot topics and pain points. Your proposal can now be tailored to include the data they want and need to give your proposal a fair hearing. It may be that each of these individuals wants some different information. You stand a better chance to get more money for a one-time expense than you do for an ongoing expense.

Resource management is not a mystical art. You are fully capable of analyzing, prioritizing, and monitoring your school resources. Remember to align the school's allotments and expenditures with priorities in the school improvement plan. Finally, remember that there are frequently unspent funds which you can tap into by aligning your requests with the district level priorities.

5
Managing Individuals

Shawntee Stevens (not her real name) has been principal of a middle school with over 75 faculty and staff and over 900 students. She also served as a central office program specialist and as a senior level administrator.

Being a principal is fundamentally different from any other role in the school system. You must change your mind-set from being an individual contributor to one who is effective in making things happen with other people. As an assistant principal, you were helping other people, but you were also tasked with being an individual contributor. Ideally, many central office jobs are designed to support the work of either the school or the superintendent. As a principal, you create a sense of shared ownership among the teachers, staff, parents, community, and students. You also have to be able to assess individual member's strengths and find the right role for each person. You have to allow teachers to use their strengths as well as help the school to achieve the school's annual goals. It is a very different mind-set in terms of how you manage individuals. We talk in schools about differentiating instruction for different students with different needs. The same holds true with your faculty and staff. You have to learn what their strengths and weaknesses are and then find ways to leverage their strengths while minimizing their weaknesses. It's like teaching on a different level.

One of Shawntee's key points is that you have to think and work with your team as individuals. While this is difficult, there are some frameworks and tools you can use to differentiate your management of people. You differentiate based upon the task, their strengths, and their needs. You can use these frameworks to get the most out of your faculty and staff.

Leading the Individual

Effective managers employ these following strategies that encourage and enable individuals to reach a level of high performance.

"Skill and Will" Management

Skill and will management is based upon Vroom's Contingency Theory and popularized in the 1980s by Robert Hersey and Ken Blanchard (2009). Skill and will management suggests that your management behaviors shift based upon the person's:

- competence in successfully completing the task

- willingness to complete the task

This model can help you manage individuals more effectively. You manage an individual who has never done a certain type of task differently than you would an individual who is an expert at the task. For example, look at two different teachers, Steve and Helen. Steve is fresh out of college. He is your prototypical Gen Y teacher: adept at social networking and excited about using technology as a teaching tool. Helen is a Baby Boomer, a master teacher, and the department chair for her department. She has 25 years of experience and has served on several district level curriculum committees.

Steve wants to succeed but doesn't have any experience connecting lesson plans to unit plans. He is also unclear on how to link lesson and unit plans to your district curriculum competencies and standards. Steve has never created a unit or annual pacing guide. Your interactions with him and managing him will be much more directive than they will be for Helen, who would resent the intrusion. Steve, who has low skill in this area but high will (enthusiasm), needs more direction from you or a mentor. He needs to have the task broken down into small parts with frequent feedback to help him gain a sense of accomplishment and success. He also needs frequent feedback to build his confidence in creating lesson plans, unit plans, pacing guides, and linking them back to the curriculum standards. However, Steve will bristle if you try to tell him how to use the technology. In fact, he can probably give tutorials to the entire staff on how to effectively leverage the power of technology to differentiate classroom instruction for low and high achieving students.

If you try to manage Helen for the same task (aligning lesson and unit plans) the same way you managed Steve, you would likely get rebellion, distrust, or a complete disregard for you and your leadership. Helen is a master teacher and does this kind of work with creativity and flair. She constantly looks out for more effective and better ways to get students to learn the content. Her skill (high) and will (high) strongly suggests leaving her alone as long as she continues to get the results you expect. Your customized management strategy for her consists of ensuring that you tell her periodically how important she is to the students and her positive impact on students and faculty. If Helen, however, is not very competent in technology, you should be increasingly involved in providing direction and support.

Two key points in managing based upon skill and will are:

1. Focus on the specific task: a person does not have the same level of skill and will for everything that they do.

2. When a person's skill is low, they need direction. When their will is low, they need support.

Performance Management and Metrics

Lawler (2008) suggests that one pillar of effective performance management is defining performance. Determining *what* needs to be done and *how to* do it is the bedrock for performance management. Fortunately, most school executives have this foundation in place when looking at the evaluation instruments for teachers, teacher assistants, assistant principals, guidance counselors, and staff. Staff evaluation instruments provide a foundation or starting point for monitoring performance. If you don't have these evaluation instruments, take the time to talk and get some evaluation instruments from your colleagues. To get to the next level of high performance, however, you need to ensure that the objectives are clearly identified and that key drivers are clearly outlined.

Key drivers are those actions, behaviors, knowledge, and skill that the best performers do on a consistent basis. Key drivers will make your performance measure go up or down. For example, you may decide to focus upon student engagement as a key driver for student academic performance. You believe that having high levels of student engagement will translate into higher student achievement. A key driver in this case would be student engagement. Once you have determined what actions will make that key driver go up or down, you determine how to measure that key driver and then set specific, measurable, ambitious, relevant, and time-bound goals to achieve it.

Returning to our example of high student engagement, you may decide that high student engagement is 95% or more of the students actively attending to the instructional activity. Ninety-five percent becomes the metric for student engagement. Ideally, you should have a small number of key drivers (no more than 5). Finally, you set up meetings to check on how each group is doing on that key driver (Cable, 2007). For example, as in our example of Steve, you may have some key actions such as creating unit plans with specific objectives for each unit tied directly to the district objectives.

Another phrase for key drivers is the idea of "Success Enablers." Barry Zweibel, an executive coach in Chicago (www.ggci.com) suggests that the more clearly you can communicate your thoughts on key drivers, the more likely it is that your faculty and staff will incorporate them into their daily work. Success enablers should be aligned with your performance appraisal instruments.

Success Enabler Examples

You may have success enablers for your secretarial and administrative support staff such as the following:

♦ Consistently use what you know, learn, and master to make existing processes and procedures more efficient and focused on the students, teachers, and parents.

♦ Always serve as a positive ambassador with every interaction with internal and external clients.

♦ Consistently monitor your areas of responsibility to head off and solve small problems before they escalate into larger, more difficult, and more urgent issues.

For your assistant principals, some success enablers may be:

- Consistently update you with equal speed and clarity on good and bad news.

- Come to you with well thought out recommendations to resolve a problem before it escalates.

- Consistently anticipate how issues and actions can have a cascading effect and take steps to proactively manage those effects.

- Consistently schedule daily debriefing meetings at the start or end of the day (or attend the 5-minute stand-up meetings outlined in chapter 10, "Making Meetings Work").

For your teachers, success enablers may be:

- Treat every child with respect, dignity, and high expectations for academic success.

- Proactively keep parents involved as supportive partners.

- Consistently work within your grade level to find ways to make each child academically successful.

Work-Life Balance

Nobody goes into teaching thinking that the profession comes with a 40-hour work week where you can clock in and clock out. Teacher work has long hours including phone calls to parents, e-mails to return, papers to grade, and lesson and unit plans to prepare—all while trying to balance personal and family life. If you spend 60–70 hours per week, your assistant principals may either follow your lead or shut down. They may decide that working for you is so consuming that they need to find another place where they can follow their passion while maintaining some type of work-life balance. This is especially important for the Baby Boomers, Gen X, and Gen Y teachers in your school. Some savvy principals make explicit what they expect regarding e-mails (normal hours for checking and responding to e-mails and protecting them from parents who expect an instantaneous response). These principals give these expectations to the faculty and to parents (within 48 hours for e-mail). These savvy principals also set up systems for e-mail and phone messages reminding parents and other community members that:

- If there is an emergency, call the school number and label it urgent, rather than send an e-mail.

- Teachers will not be checking their e-mail on the weekends and holidays.

They also help their teachers on work days by encouraging them to take time to visit and network with their colleagues during extended lunch times. They also remind faculty to go home at a decent hour. Today's faculty and staff may well be juggling their children, advancing their education, and taking care of their parents, in addition to their work and other family obligations. Finding ways to help them take a breath and know that work-life balance is important to sustained success goes a long way toward building the trusting relationship of today's school principal.

Special Types of Employees

If you take a candid look at your faculty and staff (without looking at what you have put on their performance appraisals), you will likely get a three-part distribution: high performers, good solid middle performers, and few (one hopes) underperformers. Unfortunately, many school leaders get sucked into spending most of their time with the underperformers. They try to help the underperformers get better or document their performance for action plans or dismissal. You run the risk of increased employee turnover if you completely ignore the other two groups. High performing people tend to want to be surrounded by other high performing people and middle performers link in with these high performers. If you don't have a good solid group of both high and middle performers, you may well have more difficulty hiring high performers. This is especially true in schools with a historic pattern of low performance. Recent pay and bonuses paid for teachers who work in these schools (derisively called "combat pay") are not bringing in or keeping the talent that they were designed to recruit and retain. Here are some examples of different types of employees and some strategies you can use to manage and lead them more effectively.

High Performers

Bill Gates noted that "if you take my top twenty people, Microsoft becomes a very mediocre company overnight." You see Gates' comment in action when a high performing teacher resigns. When you lose a very high performing teacher, parents ask:

+ Why did she leave? (especially if it was to another school)

+ Who are you are going to hire in her place?

You now have a bull's-eye on both your back and the new teacher's back until the new teacher proves herself. If the new teacher doesn't immediately perform at a high level, the teacher can be unfairly criticized, and you begin hearing whispers about your inability to hire and keep good faculty. This distraction can also have a negative impact on other teachers and staff. It could lead to even more high performing teachers and staff leaving. It's in your best interest to find ways to keep your high performing people with you.

One survey found that the number one motivator for high performing and high potential employees to stay passionate about their jobs was job fulfillment and challenge (Vermi, Greenslade, and Armatys, 2008). They wanted to work on projects that they considered challenging, intellectually stimulating, or strategically consequential. These high performers get easily frustrated when think they are underutilized. They also found that being linked to results was also a key driver in motivating them.

How might you use this information for your high performing faculty and staff? Let's take an example with some of your top performing teachers. In some schools, the neediest students are given to the least experienced teachers who are often first year or lateral entry teachers coming from another profession. The most experienced and strongest teachers are given the students who are relatively easy to teach. This dynamic fails both the students and the teachers. The students get shortchanged, the new teachers tend to resign within 2 years, and the most experienced teachers end up cruising along teaching only the most advanced courses or "retiring on the job." Strong school principals address this issue using a blend of strategies:

- Appeal to the high performing teacher by asking her to take, along with the high achieving classes, one or two classes of the students who most need her skills.

- Have the high performing teacher mentor the new teacher (who can teach an advanced level class).

- Share unit and lesson plans among grade levels or departments for that advanced class.

Frame your conversations with these high performing teachers in a way that motivates them. Simply telling them they are going to teach a different level class without helping them understand the context can be disastrous. Instead, link their strong performance to the overall school need and appeal to their competence and the challenge (linking to school results) to help this group of students succeed.

Middle Performers

If you spend your time focusing upon only the low performers, you may end up losing the middle performers who aspire to be regarded as high performing. Martin Cozyn, vice president of human resources, at Nortel Networks, notes, "You need to know who your top people are but you also have to watch out for the message you are sending because a disenfranchised middle can be as damaging to your business as the loss of all of your top talent" (Stuart, 2005).

Here are some proven strategies to nurture and reward middle performers.

Step 1—Manage the Message: If you call your middle performers "average" or have as your performance indicator "meets expectations," you may have a message problem. If you ask people to rate themselves as high potential or average, almost everybody will consider themselves high potential. Simply changing the middle category to something like "performs well" helps deliver the message that middle performers fully meet every performance indicator within a performance area. One school system has moved to a three-tier performance indicator—"consistently outperforms," "performs well," and "fails to meet expectations."

Step 2—Broaden and align recognition programs: Recognition programs are a common tool to motivate people. Yet, you may end up rewarding a behavior that you are trying to thwart if the recognition programs are not aligned. Let's take improved teamwork as a performance measure. If you are working on improving teamwork, but your recognition program focuses upon individual contributors (teacher of the month, employee of the month/quarter), you end up sabotaging what you are trying to reward. Instead, look at creating recognition structures that are based upon a standard, rather than competing against each other. The cosmetics company, Mary Kay Inc., is one of the most effective companies in the world at using standards based performance. Mary Kay Inc. has multiple categories where people have a chance to not only compete as a team but also compete against themselves. You might adapt their approach for student achievement. Let's assume you have quarterly assessments to analyze where students are and how well they have achieved. In addition, you have some adequate yearly progress (AYP) targets for subgroups. You make teachers aware of the link between performance on quarterly assessments and improved performance on the end-of-the-year tests that are used to determine AYP. You also set up and monitor systems where your teachers work in grade-level or departmental groups, collaboratively analyzing the test questions and concepts that are giving the students the most difficulty. They then set up strategies to remediate or more effectively teach the concepts. At quarterly assessment time, you can have multiple categories for the subgroups that you are focusing on, such as these:

+ highest percentage passing

+ greatest growth between quarters

+ greatest growth percentage overall for each of the grade levels or departments

These recognition programs focus on team rather than individual growth. This helps align both your goal of increasing teamwork and linking performance to effort.

Step 3—Differentiate reward structures: Today's workers are used to an almost limitless variety of choices. It seems as if people are overburdened with choices, ranging from types of cereal in the grocery store to the channels they can use to view TV and listen to music. If you use only one type of reward, then people may feel cheated and less valued as individuals. You don't need a limitless number of options, but you can work with your faculty and staff to generate some ideas for rewards for a job well done. You might consider nonfinancial rewards, such as these:

+ special projects

+ exposure to senior executives or leadership on district level committees

+ mini-grants from school funds or Parent Teacher Organizations grants($100–$250) for grade levels to try something innovative or as a reward for good performance

+ additional professional development opportunities

+ book store gift cards

+ gift certificates from your local business partners or chamber of commerce

Ask your team what they think would serve as a motivating reward for either individuals or teams. The more they buy into the idea, the harder they'll work, and the better chance you have of fielding a team where everybody is helping each other achieve the organizational goals.

Under-Performers

When you have an underperforming employee, the first step is to identify the problem behavior(s) that prevents the person from being more productive. You have to quickly confront the behavior in a way that focuses on that specific behavior (not the personality), treat the individual as an adult, and focus on how to improve professional knowledge and skills. Clarify the changes you expect from this point forward. It is important that your conversation with the employee focuses on the specific behavior. Be sure to end the conversation with an action plan that holds the employee accountable.

Discussions of this sort, however, need to be done in private. The cliché of "praise in public, discipline in private" is applicable in confronting problem behavior. Here is a model that you can use in preparing for your conversations with your employees.

1. *Be specific:* Describe the specifics of the situation and the problem you saw. The problem can come from an observation that you have made or a verified complaint from a parent. Discuss the actual inappropriate behavior clearly and concisely. Focusing on the specific facts helps the employee put the issue into context, shows where the issue is, and helps maintain the focus on behavior rather than on personality traits.

2. *Focus on the issue and why it is a problem:* You have to candidly share the issue and why it is a problem as it relates to the school , school values, and school norms. The problem may be based on your expectations of how others are treated, on your expectations for the classroom and for instruction, or upon the norms and values that you have for people within your organization.

3. *Listen:* We've all been guilty of getting ready to have a candid conversation with someone without having all of the facts. Sometimes, we learn there was another side to the issue that we didn't see in our anger-induced haze. We then get the reputation of not being willing to listen. Avoid this perception by asking the person why in her view, this happened. You can't resolve the problem if you don't know the other person's side of the story.

4. *Outline expectations:* There is a problem. You've outlined the problem from your perspective. You've heard the other person's perspective. You now need to share your expectations for this type of behavior. Again, these should be specific and behavior-based.

5. *Ask for ideas on how to solve while offering your support:* McKenna and Maister (2002) suggest that for any solution to have a chance of success, the individual must fully accept that the problem is his, not yours or anyone else's. Any solution has to be a solution that he buys into, rather than half-heartedly accepting your imposed solution. It is important to ask questions like "Will what you are proposing move

toward solving what we discussed?" and "How will we be able to tell whether this proposed solution will really work?" at the same time you offer support and encouragement by offering resources and contact people. But avoid taking the next step toward finding the solution to the problem. You may, in offering your encouragement, call someone who might be able to help them. Make that call while the individual is in your office; then have the individual continue with the next steps.

6. *Set an action plan with metrics and set a follow-up date:* You may not need this step with less crucial problems. However, if this is an important issue, you need to have the individual decide on an action plan that has clear deadlines and measures of performance. When you put the next step on the calendar in the presence of the employee, it sends a powerful message that you treat this as an important issue. One principal notes, "This plan has to be explicit and in writing. It's almost like law."

It's always a good idea to prepare for a meeting like this. The worksheet on the following page, Figure 5.1, can help you collect your thoughts before talking to the employee. Jot down your notes and thoughts before you meet. This process helps you clarify the issue, why it is a problem, and what you want the employee to do differently. Don't bring this into your meeting with the employee. Instead, bring note paper and your calendar to take notes and to mark the follow-up date on your calendar. After the meeting, follow up with an e-mail to confirm key discussion points and outlining the action based plan.

Leading Prima Donnas

Have you been held hostage by a prima donna? Prima donnas enjoy notoriety in the community and support from many parents. Innovative, effective, and creative in the classroom, they get all of their students to perform at their best. Prima donnas are also cranky, arrogant, and think the rules apply to everybody but them. Prima donnas may implicitly (or explicitly) say that if things don't go their way, they will leave the school. They may be belligerent, defensive, and generally intimidate others with their superior attitude. Prima donnas can hold even the most experienced and wise principal hostage because of their performance. And that's the rub. The clear distinction between an employed and unemployed arrogant, belligerent individual can be defined in three words: *consistent high performance.* Almost every manager will be confronted with a prima donna (or prima don—gender doesn't matter here). Your prima donna could be a teacher, a technology expert, or your secretary.

Working with a prima donna is difficult because you want to reward what this consistently high performing individual does that causes the positive results while not rewarding the prima donna's preening habits, which have been groomed and refined over the years. Here are some strategies you might use to help manage consistently high performing prima dons and donnas. Two filters that can help in managing these individuals are "Ethics and Policy" and "Performance."

FIGURE 5.1   Problem Behavior Pre-Meeting Notes

Problem Behavior Pre-Meeting Notes

1. What was the problem (be specific and concrete. What happened? When did it happen?)

2. Why is the issue a problem? (ethics, policy, poor behavior-not personality)

3. What are your expectations? (be specific on what and by when)

4. How can the staff member improve and meet expectations?

♦ *Ethics and Policy:* This should be your first filter. Is this person violating any ethical canons or school board policy? If donna or don is violating either of these, you have no choice but to confront and quickly use whatever disciplinary measures you have to in accordance with your local and state policies and procedures. For example, it's important for a teacher to care about the children under the teacher's supervision; it is likely illegal or against board policy for the teacher to dispense pain medications without a note from a parent or medical professional. It is important for a technology teacher to show how streaming video websites work; it is likely against board policy for the technology teacher to temporarily disable your school system's website filtering system without following your district policies. You have to handle this person in the exact same manner as any other employee regardless of whether the person is teacher of the year or a family member of the school board chair.

♦ *Performance:* You have a much easier decision if the individual is not giving you consistent high performance. You should treat them as an underperformer and utilize the tools outlined for underperformers. If you have an employee who is rude to everybody and doesn't do a good job, you can and should follow your district policies and labor agreement procedures for underperformers. Each time you work with a prima donna, think through whether the person is still exhibiting consistent high performance.

First, decide if you want to spend your time and energy in managing prima donnas. Determine up front how much time, care, and feeding to spend on managing this person. Make a conscious choice on how much energy this person gets or deserves. If you simply go on a reactive basis, you have only yourself to blame. Remember that prima donnas have spent a lifetime cultivating and honing their habits. Their outstanding technical skills have overshadowed their interpersonal shortcomings, and you will have to manage your own expectations—small wins are going to be big and time-consuming.

♦ *Find the combination:* While many prima donnas exhibit the same annoying and destructive behavior, they generally have different sets of needs. Some may need additional "air time" to demonstrate their superior knowledge and intellect. Others may want public recognition for the work they have done. Still others may want to be perceived as a "power player" by being asked to serve on a district-level committee. By looking for what they want, you have a tool that you can use to help leverage better behavior from them. If your prima donna loves the limelight, and wants to be perceived as a leader, have them lead a committee, but with conditions. Your conversation may go like this. "I'm glad you've agreed to lead this committee. Remember that one of the key aspects of this committee is to get a set of recommendations that everybody will agree to. You've got a lot of skill and talent, and we need your perspective. One of the areas that will be important for you is to build on the ideas of everybody in the group. What ideas do you have to make sure that everybody is listened to and heard?" When the prima donna pushes back, you have an opening to discuss how their skills in this committee can help increase their credibility with the others on the team.

♦ *Build a wall or a fence:* Prima donnas know they are good and some may simply want to be left alone. If your prima donna simply wants to be left alone, put their expertise to use on a "lone ranger" project that aligns with your strategic goals. They don't have to spend time in what they consider wasted time in endless meetings, and you get your results.

♦ *Help the prima donna accept personal accountability:* One of the first filters you should use is consistent high performance. You can certainly include interpersonal high performance as well. If the individual is rude and inconsiderate to others and one of your key values is client service, discuss this with your prima donna. Identify the person's combination as discussed above, and then ask the individual, "How do you think others perceive you?" Point out that the prima donna runs the risk of increased alienation with the specific behaviors and actions. Serving as a mirror initiates the linkage between the prima donna's behavior and perception.

♦ *Check the "will":* You should determine the motivation behind the prima donna's behavior. It is possible that the individual believes that his/her way is the best and only way to approach the issue or professional practice. It will be important for you to listen for what is behind the approach. Is it based on sound research? Or is it rather an outgrowth of their personality and experience? If the prima donna is engaging in unprofessional behavior, however, you will need to take an entirely different approach to their behavior.

You don't want to risk creating double standards by ignoring one person's behavior while enforcing the norms of your group with the rest of your employees. A prima donna's negative effects can induce increased organizational pain and suffering as more and more schools and districts are working in small ad hoc or semipermanent teams. Unfortunately, these double standards breed resentment, lower group performance, and increase the risk of more talented and less disruptive team members moving to another school or district.

Leading Technical Professionals

The term *geek* (someone who is adept with technology) has changed from a derogatory term to a term of honor and distinction. If you have ever had a computer or cell phone go dark, you understand that knowing a geek is crucial to your short-term success and productivity. Yet, how do you manage and lead these people? Are they really different from the rest of us mere mortals? Technical professionals want the same reinforcers that nontechnical professionals want, but there can be subtleties to leading those with an engineering bent.

Technical professionals see themselves as problem solvers. They think very logically and sequentially. The technical professional is not trying to be a smart aleck by giving you a very detailed and precise answer to exactly the general question that you asked. You must have a level of precision with your questioning to get to the answer. One strategy you might use after they have answered your initial question is to ask something like, "So what am I missing that will likely come back and bite me?" As problem solvers, technical professionals look logically at whether you are part of the problem or part of the solution. If you are perceived as part of the problem or as a roadblock, technical professionals will come up with creative ways to work around you. Tech professionals love to make an impact. They love recognition, and they want to get credit for their accomplishments. Like your high performers, technical professionals are more motivated by the challenge and value being thought of as the expert.

Look for volunteers rather than simply mandate that something has to be done and be sure to avoid getting into the details of *how* the task or project needs to be achieved. Rather, focus your efforts helping them understand *what* needs to happen, within *what* parameters, and by *what* date. (See the section on delegation in chapter 2.)

As we outlined these characteristics, we hope you notice that technical professionals are no different from any faculty and staff. They want to know that their efforts will lead to a successful outcome and that they will get the credit for the success.

Our fictional principal at the start of this chapter was correct. People are individuals and expect to be treated as such. In addition, they expect the principal to not only personalize his management style to meet their needs but to recognized their unique skills and contributions to the betterment of the school.

6

Leading the Multigenerational Faculty

You have just been appointed principal to a school of 900 students with a staff of 40 teachers and 12 support personnel. One of the first things with which you are confronted is the assignment of teachers to grades, teams, and departments. As you scan the list of staff members, you begin to consider how to make assignments that will maximize people's abilities and experience and, at the same time, create effective teams. You become aware that you have a significant number, around 40% of the staff, who have 20 plus years of classroom experience. Many of those teachers "came with the bricks" and are approaching or eligible for retirement. Ranging in age from early 40s to early 60s, these teachers are the mainstays of the school and represent the traditions to which the community has become accustomed. The fact that this is your first principalship at age 38 will not be in your favor when working with the senior members of the staff. They have seen principals come and go and feel that they are the glue that holds the school together. In fact, you admit to yourself, they have provided stability in good times and bad.

Teachers with 10 to 19 years are the next group that draws your attention. This portion of the staff represents some of the strongest, most committed teachers in the school. They appear to be willing to try new approaches and agree to leadership roles when asked, especially if the position includes compensation, additional training, or increased flexibility in their schedule. Some have children enrolled in the school and appear to be ready to accept you as the new leader of the school. Now for the bad news, this is the smallest group of teachers, representing only 25% of the total staff.

The final group of teachers, 35% of the overall staff, includes a wide mix of experience and ages. This group has 0 to 10 years experience and reflects both promise and challenge for the future of the school, not to mention *your* long-term success in this school. Some are novice teachers fresh out of college; others are lateral entry to the teaching profession from other careers. You feel personally committed to the inexperienced teachers because you were responsible for bringing them into the school. If some in this group do not return next year, it could be perceived as bad judgment or lack of support on the part of the new principal. On a positive note, you are pleased to find a fair number of teachers in the 4- to 6-year span. They are bright, energetic, and eager to learn. It will be important to earn the support and confidence of this contingent early in your tenure. You will need them to do some of the heavy lifting to keep the school functioning and supervise the myriad of day-to-day activities. The flip side for this group —they are young and mobile. If they don't like the working conditions or school culture, they will be gone in 2 years or less.

So you are faced with the same dilemma that all school leaders encounter; how should I lead this multigenerational faculty, and how can I get them to work together?

Generational Differences

The distribution of age groups in our vignette mirrors the breakdown of age groups in the overall teaching workforce. If you have not thought about the implications for how you approach your staff as a group and as individuals, you need to! School executives need to be aware of the shifting demographics of the workforce and the implications for recruitment, retention, and leading a multigenerational staff of teachers. First, it will be helpful for you to become familiar with the characteristics and needs of employees in the workforce based on their age and the traits displayed by many people in those generations. Before you can develop a strategy for leading a multigenerational staff, it is necessary to understand these separate generations. This brief primer compiled from Martin and Tulgan (2006) will introduce you to the different cohorts under consideration.

Baby Boomers

The largest demographic group in the workforce, 41.5%, has been labeled the Baby Boomers. Also referred to as the "Woodstock" generation, many of the Boomers came of age during the 1970s, the decade following the Woodstock Music and Art Fair. The festival was held in August 1969 on a dairy farm in rural New York State and featured 32 of the most popular recording artists of the time. The event came to represent many of the attitudes and desires of this generation. Those who weren't there, wanted to be. The products of a child-centered upbringing, the young Boomers were ready to rebel against the safe world created by their parents. This generation also remembers the assassinations of three national leaders: President John F. Kennedy, his brother Senator Robert Kennedy, and The Reverend Martin Luther King. Ask most Boomers and they can probably tell you when and where they were when they first heard of the death of those American icons (Martin & Tulgan, 2006).

This generation was also influenced by the Vietnam War and the Watergate Scandal. These events led to antiwar protests and a general mistrust of those in authority. Much of the unrest took place on college campuses where Boomers now hold positions in administration, research, and classrooms. These experiences create a stark contrast to the attitudes that now define baby boomers; it is interesting to consider how this generation has come full circle. See Figure 6.1.

FIGURE 6.1　Baby Boomers (1946–1964) At A Glance

- ◆ American soldiers returning home from World War II created an explosion of births.

- ◆ During the Baby Boomer years, approximately 76 million Americans were born. Today, this represents 28 percent of the American population.

- ◆ The peak year was 1957 when 4.3 million babies were born in the U.S., more than any year before or since.

- ◆ Of ages 44–62 in 2008, there are 61.5 million in the workforce.

- ◆ 34% of Baby Boomers are caring for a parent or loved one.

- ◆ Half of all Boomers over 45 years old have children under 18 at home.

- ◆ Approximately 330 Baby Boomers in the United States turn 60 every hour.

From *Managing the Generation Mix* (pp. 21–27) by Martin and Tulgan, 2006, Amherst: HRD Press.

Boomers' Attitudes About Work

Reality hit the Boomers head-on when it was time to get a job and start their careers. They took off their bell-bottom jeans with holes in the knees, traded their tie-dyed T-shirts for business attire, and cut their hair. Their parents were their role models for how to get ahead in business. The parents of most Baby Boomers worked for the same company for 30 to 40 years. Baby Boomers entered the workforce with the same expectations: hard work and loyalty to the company will provide a safe and secure career to support my family.

In 1973, just as many of the Boomers were heading to work, the United States experienced a downturn in the economy due in large part to a shortage of gasoline. They remember waiting in gas lines on even or odd days, determined by the last digit of your license number, to purchase a few gallons of gas. The good old days of paying 28 cents per gallon were over. Boomers got the message however. Find a job and do your best to hold on to it.

By the mid-1980s, Baby Boomers became established in their careers and started young families. The oldest members of the generation had just turned 40 while the largest group, those born around 1957, were approaching 30 years of age. Boomers were then hit with downsizing as companies laid off thousands of workers and severely cut middle-level and executive positions. For the first time in their brief careers, Boomers were forced into job-hopping or changing their career paths all together. This phenomenon is particularly important because their younger siblings or children, Generation X, were taking it all in at home. This would play a significant role in how the next generation would approach their careers and their thoughts on job security. Boomers were forced to become free agents or become first-time entrepreneurs in order to survive. See Figure 6.2 for Baby Boomer statistics.

FIGURE 6.2   Baby Boomers by the Numbers

Veteran teachers with 20 or more years in the classroom are the largest age group of teachers in the teaching work force. A survey by the National Association of Educators in 2001 found that 38% of teachers in the United States had 20 or more years of teaching (*Status of the American Public School Teacher, 2000-2001*, NEA). The U.S. Department of Education stated in their annual report to Congress in 2007 that 29% of the teaching work force was between 50 and 59 years of age. Teachers age 60 and above made up 4% of all teachers included in the *Schools and Staffing Survey*. Those two groups represented 33% of the teaching work force in 2007 (*Livingston, 2007*, U.S. Department of Education, National Center for Education Statistics).

How To Lead Baby Boomers in Schools

If you were part of that dynamic generation, perhaps you enjoyed the walk down memory lane. If, however, you are like the 38-year-old principal whom we met at the beginning of the chapter, you will want to be open to their insights and discussing the experiences that have made an impact on their lives. You will start to gain additional insight into why Boomers approach life and their work in unique ways. The one thing that you do not want to do is ignore them. Authors Carolyn Martin and Bruce Tulgan interviewed thousands of people for their book, *Managing the Generation Mix*, including a 50-something elementary school teacher who said,

> Our principal is falling all over Gen Yers, who I agree are sharp. But in the process, she's discounting the Boomer teachers who have made this school great and who could serve as mentors to these young people. What she doesn't know is, Yers are going to leave for other opportunities because her leadership is so poor. They are all 'flash and dash.' We will still be here. And we are not happy. (2006, p. 31)

Pay attention to this group. Unless your school has opened in the last 10 years, this is probably the largest group of teachers in the school, and they are very well connected to the community. The senior members can help you understand the politics of the system and its surroundings. The teachers with 20 or more years of experience were there before you arrived, and many of them will still be there when you move to your next position. They most certainly will still be living in the community, and some may get elected to the school board. This same group may be seen as holding the school back from adopting new practices, but you cannot afford to have them working against you or leaving in large numbers. The Boomers will not be replaced easily, and you need time to train the next generation of teachers to take leadership roles and mentor the young teachers just coming on board.

Here are five tips from Martin and Tulgan (2006, p. 33) for our young principal, or principals of any age, for working with Baby Boomers:

- Honor their historical memory.
- Give them recognition.

- ♦ Let them try out new ideas.

- ♦ Help bridge the team-individual divide.

- ♦ Coach and challenge.

Let's consider what that might look like in a school environment.

1. Principals should honor their historical memory: Invite the Baby Boomers on the staff to talk about what they have experienced during their tenure at the school and in their careers. They have seen a lot of students come and go, and gaining a better appreciation for their perspective will help you value their contributions. It will be helpful to know if any of the staff members were part of the original school as a teacher or even as a student. They may not reveal their age, but they are proud of their loyalty to the school. Martin and Tulgan heard one high school teacher describe himself and his colleagues as the "dinosaurs" in their department.

> We just trudge along following and enforcing the rules and regulations. Our out-of-school lives are quite limited. We put in the extra hours and give stability to the department. We're the first to arrive and the last to leave. We're cynical, yet we're the most loyal to the school. (p. 27)

You probably know one or more teachers who might make a similar statement. We are left to speculate on why some teachers would characterize themselves as cynical. But the key word in the statement is "loyalty," and the challenge is how to build on the loyalty that veteran teachers feel for their school. According to Martin and Tulgan, the first step is to honor their memory of school traditions and *why things are done the way they are around here.* We have found that once the senior members of a team or department feel honored and respected for their contributions, they become less cynical. That takes us to the next step in leading Baby Boomers.

2. Principals should give Baby Boomers recognition: Everyone likes to be recognized, but it would be easy to overlook the more seasoned and experienced members of your staff. The tendency is to focus on the young teachers who might be struggling and need additional help. Teachers who are approaching the top of the salary schedule and having no plans for changing careers need to be recognized for their continued service and contributions to the students and life of the school. Tulgan and Martin (2006) offer the following advice: "Remember that a basic way to honor your Boomers is to listen to them, individually and as a team, and genuinely factor their ideas into your decision-making process" (p. 34). The young principal from our illustration would do well to schedule a time to meet with all of the veteran teachers on the staff, one to one or in small groups, before the first day of school. Ask their observations about the strengths of the school and what needs should be addressed to improve the teaching and learning conditions for everyone. The act of listening is one of the most important ways that a leader can demonstrate respect and recognize people for their contributions.

3. Principals should let Baby Boomers try out new ideas: Boomers' deep-seated commitment to a school's history and tradition do not necessarily mean they are too stuck in their ways; many Boomers are anxious to try out new approaches and teach new material. You would be wise to give them permission to integrate new strategies and encourage them to experiment with technology in their classrooms. Experienced teachers will not take risks if they feel that you will not support them for trying something new or will be disappointed if it does not go well the first time. They may just be in a rut or need a nudge to try out an idea that they have been thinking about for some time.

4. Principals should help Baby Boomers bridge the team-individual divide: From their research, Martin and Tulgan (2006) learned that "many Boomers are driven by conflicting impulses: the urge to compete to get ahead of the pack, and the desire to lead or participate on a productive team" (p. 35). After many years of experience, we found the best approach is a personal request to senior members of the staff to share their experiences with the new and less seasoned teachers. For example, one of the authors, while serving as a high school principal, decided that the students would benefit if teachers worked together to align their instructional strategies and performance assessments within each subject area. He knew that this would not sit well with some teachers who had been allowed to operate independently for years. One conversation stands out as an example. There was a very effective and successful teacher who was assigned only Advanced Placement courses. The principal was asking all teachers in each department to work together to develop common objectives and course assessments. He knew that this experienced teacher had a lot to offer to her department and might not benefit from this type of collaboration. He also knew that other teachers were watching to see if she would attend the meetings and participate. In advance of the meeting, he went to her classroom and made a personal request that she share her expertise and assist the other members of the department in the planning process. The principal explained the goals and outcomes for student success and asked for her help. She agreed to attend the meetings and share her materials and experience with her colleagues. Teacher collaboration in her department improved and student learning and test scores made a significant improvement as well.

Do not assume that Boomers will not work with the next generation of teachers. Go and ask them for their help. The personal touch will pay off in support for your initiatives and teamwork.

5. Principals should coach and challenge: Regarding their final recommendation for leading Baby Boomers, Martin and Tulgan (2006) explain, "Become a coach who facilitates goals, not dictates them, and who challenges Boomers to grow. Remember, self-improvement is a major aspiration of this cohort" (p. 35). If you are a Baby Boomer, you will remember the self-help book, *I'm OK, You're OK*, by Thomas A. Harris, MD. First released in 1969, it made the *New York Times* Best-Seller list and has sold over 15 million copies. Chances are pretty good that the senior members of the staff read this self-help book. This is just one example of the self-improvement genre that became popular in the 1970s. Our experience confirms the advice from Martin and Tulgan; Baby Boomers want to improve but they may not want to be told how to improve. They will not respond to "command and control" orders the same way that their Veteran Generation parents might have. You will be more successful by asking Boomers to design their own professional development that aligns with the school's overall goals.

FIGURE 6.3 What Do Baby Boomers Have To Offer Your School?

> ◆ Loyalty to the school
> ◆ Teaching experience and expertise
> ◆ Knowledge of school traditions and procedures
> ◆ Valuable connections in the school's community
> ◆ Many are willing to mentor young teachers

Leading the Baby Boomers on your staff may be one of the biggest challenges you face. We will repeat, do not ignore this group. Martin and Tulgan (2006) offer sound advice:

> Since Boomers will play significant roles on your Gen Mix team for the next 5 to 15 years, you can't afford to have them remain "not happy." Most have admirable track records and a strong work ethic; many are ready to become mentors to their younger colleagues. *Unless they feel respected and recognized for their accomplishments, however, you will have little success getting them to work collaboratively.* (italics added, p. 36)

Figure 6.3 shows what Baby Boomers have to offer your school.

Generation X

Beginning in 1965, the cohort that followed the Baby Boomers has been labeled Generation X. There is a lack of consensus from writers as to the end-date for Gen X, but regardless of where that date might fall, this is a much smaller generation. The reduction in birth rate is believed to have been affected by *Roe v. Wade*, the Supreme Court decision that overturned all federal and state laws that restricted a woman's right to have an abortion. Improved birth-control methods and women going into the workforce were also factors that played a role in reducing the overall size of this generation (Gronbach, 2008). As we will examine later, this downturn in the population created a similar reduction in the workforce and teaching force as well. See Generation X At a Glance, Figure 6.4.

There are several factors that had an influence on Generation X. The emergence of new technologies has been a big part of this generation's development. This group grew up playing games on hand-held devices and a wide range of interactive games that could be plugged into their televisions at home. They did not have to go out to the arcades and pay 50 cents for a 5-minute game—they owned them at home. The computer industry was the new frontier for young people looking for business opportunities and for control over their careers. Think Michael Dell, poster child for Generation X. Born in 1965, he started PC Limited out of his dorm room while at the University of Texas-Austin. At the age of 19, he dropped out of college to focus his energies on running his own company, which later became Dell Computers. In 1992, Dell became the youngest CEO of a Fortune

FIGURE 6.4   Generation X (1965–1984) At A Glance

- Total of 69 million live births from 1965 to 1984.
- Smaller than Baby Boomer generation due to Roe v. Wade and improved birth-control methods.
- Also called "latchkey kids"; mothers went to work and no one was at home after school.
- High rate of divorce for parents of Gen X
- Comfortable with technology

From *The Age Curve* (pp. 255–257) by Kenneth W. Gronbach, 2008, New York: AMACOM.

500 Company, and in 2009 at age 44 ranks no. 25 in the top list of billionaires with an estimated wealth of 12.3 billion dollars (Kroll, Miller, & Serafin, 2009). Not bad for a college dropout.

The changing role of institutions also had an impact of how Generation X views the world and forced them to develop survival skills. Their generation saw divorce rates soar and a sharp increase in the number of dual income families. Children left at home to care for themselves and younger brothers or sisters were referred to as latchkey kids. This generation also saw their parents abandon some of the traditional institutions such as churches, schools, and devotion to employers that Baby Boomers experienced from their parents (Martin & Tulgan, 2001).

Attitudes About Work

Generation X witnessed the rise and fall of many public and private corporations played out in the media and saw their parents downsized and lose their pensions and benefits. In their 2005 article, "If I Pass the Baton, Who Will Grab It?," Lancaster and Stillman observed that Generation Xers are:

> skeptical of large institutions and uncomfortable with layers of bureaucracy. By the age of 20, Generation Xers had already watched 23,000 hours of television. And in the media, they saw every major American institution called into question, from the presidency to the military, to organized religion, to corporate America, and yes, even state and local governments. Too many Xers think if you can name the institution, they can name the crime. (p. 8)

Generation X realized that job security was a thing of the past. If they were going to be successful, Gen X understood that they would have to be responsible for their own careers. The climate of uncertainty in the 1980s created a free agent mind-set that plays a role in how Gen X approaches work and their careers.

Growth in the technology sector and the economic boom of the 1990s led to increased career opportunities for this cohort of young professionals. Gen Xers were eager to sign on with small start-up companies that did not do business as usual. Students coming out of college were offered signing bonuses and job titles to match.

The mind-set of free agency and increased opportunities for college graduates did not steer many Gen Xers in the direction of teaching. At the same time, schools were experiencing a drop in enrollment and little mobility from Baby Boomers already well-established in their schools. Job opportunities were available in large numbers in new careers, and college graduates sought those opportunities instead of entering teaching. See Generation X By The Numbers, Figure 6.5.

FIGURE 6.5   Generation X by the Numbers

In 2003-2004, teachers between the ages of 30 to 39 (Gen-X)represented only 24% of the teaching force compared to teachers who were 40 years of age or older (Baby Boomers) who comprised 54% of full-time teachers. There are not enough Gen-X teachers to replace the Boomers who have retired in the last five years or will leave in the next ten years. School districts will be forced to hire new teachers (Gen-Y) as they graduate from college.

From *The conditions of education 2007 in brief* (p. 17), by A. Livingston, 2007, U.S. Department of Education. Washington, DC: National Center for Education Statistics.

How To Lead Generation X in Schools

The 38-year-old principal in our opening case study should be able to relate to this group of teachers, ages 30 to 40. This age group in our hypothetical school *mirrors the size of this age group nationally* at 24% of the teaching force reported in the annual report of the National Center for Education Statistics *Conditions of Education 2007* (2007). Our principal will need to incorporate the following strategies to help motivate and retain teachers in this small but significant group.

1. Principals should be open to flexible teaching assignments and arrangements.

Generation X teachers want to create a balance between work and life outside of school. Sometimes their desire for balance is misunderstood as lack of commitment or work ethic. Many of these young teachers do not want to repeat the same mistakes of their parents—over emphasis on work and little time for family. We recommend that principals be open to accommodating requests for late arrival or the need to attend functions at school for those with young children. For example, if the standard report time for teachers is 7:00 a.m. but the daycare center does not accept drop-offs until that time, then the teacher has a real dilemma. It would relieve stress to give him or her first-period planning or switch morning duties for lunch or after school responsibilities. Teachers with students in elementary school would like to go to special events or eat lunch occasionally with their kids but might be afraid to ask permission. Job sharing is also a popular way of creating flexible time for the balance between work and family.

2. Principals should provide opportunities for continuous professional development.

Generation X is focused on improving professional skills and knowledge as a means of managing their careers. The Baby Boomers may not see the need for those afterschool workshops, but Gen X will be there on the front row. Remember, this group believes that they are free agents, and if they don't need the strategies and skills right away—not a problem, their next employer might expect them. Gen X does not want to get behind, and they want to be ready to assume more responsibilities.

3. Principals should open doors for increased responsibilities and leadership opportunities.

Gen X is a much smaller group of employees who have been waiting in the wings for a chance to move into leadership roles held by the much larger group of Baby Boomer employees. Gen X is outnumbered and follows a generation of teachers who are still on the job. (Refer to By the Numbers.) Principals will need to look for ways to increase responsibilities and challenge the group of teachers with 10 to 15 years of experience. If you don't, they may look for those opportunities in other schools or even other careers. Martin and Tulgan, (2006) believe that:

> Responsibility is the proving ground that you trust them, have confidence in them, and recognize their growth and development. In fact, for this cohort, increasing responsibility is what makes them feel empowered. Deprived of that empowerment, they'll walk over to your competitor. (p. 48)

These are your school leaders of the future. You need to get them involved today.

4. Principals should encourage the use of instructional technology.

Keep in mind that Generation X grew up with video games and computers. The Baby Boomers used slide rulers and manual typewriters while this generation had handheld calculators and word processing. They are not only comfortable with technology, they expect it. We noticed a trend as we interviewed prospective teachers starting around 1995. Young teachers coming out of school wanted to know what technology would be available in the school and if their students would have access for instruction. Schools need to continue to update computers and instructional technology and involve teachers in the selection of the equipment and software. Technology is also another way of giving Gen X more responsibility and recognition for instructional integration and training their colleagues. See what Gen Xers have to offer your school, Figure 6.6.

Figure 6.6   What Does Gen X Have To Offer Your School?

- ♦ Eager to participate in professional development and learn new teaching skills
- ♦ Accept accountability measures more easily than Baby Boomers
- ♦ Understand the need to collaborate with colleagues to improve overall performance
- ♦ Will accept and expect direct criticism more easily than Gen-Y

From *Millennials and K-12 Schools* (pp. 102–106) by Neil Howe and William Strauss, 2008, Great Falls, VA: Life Course Associates

Generation Y

Generation Y, the children of Baby Boomers, is projected to exceed their parents' generation and grow to 100 million by 2010. If Gen X feels comfortable with technology, Gen Y has it in their DNA. By the time they entered middle school, they had the Internet, e-mail, and their own cell phones. They think that they have all the answers, and if they don't, they just can just search for the information on Google. Gen Y also wants to know all about you and doesn't mind revealing information about them; just check out their Facebook page. They are used to being on the go, balancing soccer practice, piano lessons, and school homework while riding in the family minivan. Their parents doted on them and are often referred to as helicopter parents for being quick to drop in and rescue their kids at a moment's notice. This attention did not stop when they went off to college or became young adults. Gen Yers often move back home to save on expenses, plan their next move and seek their parents' help in completing their resume and finding employment. (Lancaster and Stillman, 2006) Some parents of Gen Y may not know when to let go and continue to intervene for their young adult if they think that they are getting a raw deal. Believe it! We have seen this happen.

Members of this generation are concerned about the environment, poverty, and equal access to education and are demonstrating that passion by volunteering in record numbers. Many college graduates are postponing careers or graduate school to serve a year or two in low-paying jobs with a social focus, such as the Peace Corps or Teach for America and will bring this same social consciousness to their future employment and careers.

Attitudes About Work

Growing up with access to lots of information at their finger tips, this cohort of talented, well-educated young people has also been labeled Generation "Why" (see Chester, 2002). Gen Yers want to know why you are asking them to following certain protocols and why deadlines are important. "Because the boss thinks that it is important" may work for the Baby Boomers, but not for this generation. Their experience has taught them to be skeptical

FIGURE 6.7 Generation Y (1982–2000) At A Glance

♦ Also called Millennials, Generation Next, and Generation Why

♦ 76 million live births between 1982 and 2000

♦ 32 million workers or 22 % of the workforce in 2006

♦ Technology for entertainment and personal communication has always been a part of their lives.

♦ Remember bombings in Oklahoma City, Atlanta Summer Olympics, World Trade Center, and 9/11

♦ Lived during the rise of school shootings like Columbine High School

♦ Concerned for the environment and the future

From *Managing the Generation Mix* (p. 55–57) by Carolyn Martin and Bruce Tulgan, 2006, Amherst, HRD Press.

FIGURE 6.8   Generation Y by the Numbers

The percentage of teachers under the age of 30 grew from 12% in 1993-94 to 17% in 2003–04. The total number of teachers also increased from 2.6 million to 3.3 million teachers during the same time period. Schools will have to compete for new, inexperienced teachers and work to keep them to fill their classrooms for the foreseeable future.

From *The conditions of education 2007 in brief* (p.17), by A. Livingston, 2007, Washington, DC: U.S. Department of Education, National Center for Education Statistics.

and they will expect a rationale for why they are being asked to perform in a prescribed manner. Don't be surprised when they express themselves bluntly and offer their opinions. Their parents allowed them to be involved in decision making at home and they are accustomed to giving advice, especially when it comes to technology. Martin and Tulgan (2001) put it this way, "They're more than willing to tell you how to fix our team, department, and organization even before they've completed your orientation program (p. 58)."

Gen Yers will need you to explain the workplace culture and expectations. They have traveled widely and volunteered building homes for the needy and are not impressed with titles and corporate dress. If business casual is the norm, then you will need to be clear about that expectation. They may also need coaching on how to address the leadership in your office and in the district office and when it is appropriate to do so. One 24-year-old told us, "Our college instructors didn't care about how we dressed; they were interested in what we did. Some of our professors asked us to call them by their first names and would discuss a wide range of topics over coffee. We just need to be told what is expected." They move at a fast pace with instant feedback. It will be important to check in with them frequently to listen to their concerns and let them know how they are doing. They feel comfortable challenging authority and might not understand how to get the answers that they need to stay committed (Lancaster & Stillman, 2006).

How To Lead Generation Y in Schools

1. Face-to-face time with the principal is important: The principal who wants to retain these young teachers needs to keep in mind that they received lots of feedback and attention from their parents. If you have a large staff, then you will need to delegate this role carefully and verify that the mentor/coach is interacting on a day-to-day basis with new teachers. It is not sufficient to say, "Let me know if you have any problems or need anything." That may work with teachers who have experience, but it will not be effective for Gen Yers. They need face time with the school leader and will expect it. Don't wait for the performance evaluation conference to give them needed feedback. They want to know if they are doing a good job and where they can improve (Martin & Tulgan, 2001).

2. Collaboration with coworkers is a must: Many principals have been struggling to get Baby Boomers and Gen Xers to collaborate on curriculum pacing and aligning teaching strategies. Not to worry, Gen Y will not push back on working in teams to address the

FIGURE 6.9   What Generation Y Has To Offer Your School

♦ More comfortable with diversity than older generations

♦ Flexible and adaptable to new situations

♦ Enjoy and need to collaborate with colleagues

♦ Want to be mentored by older, experienced employees

♦ Want to make an immediate contribution to the organization

From *Managing Generation Y* (p.13–15) by Carolyn Martin and Bruce Tulgan, 2001, Amherst: HRD Press.

core mission of the school. But, do not be confused; Gen Y will recognize the difference between meaningful collaboration and ancillary committee work. They are used to networking in the virtual world but also value personal interactions with colleagues. If they feel connected to and appreciated by their colleagues, they will stay (Robert Half International, 2007).

3. Gen Y will expect a coach, not a boss: Young people entering the workforce today are looking for a supervisor who serves more as a mentor and coach and less as a boss. If you want them to be committed and loyal, you will need to earn their respect, not for your position, but for your expertise and willingness to guide them in developing their craft. From a survey of young employees, Robert Half International reports that "working with a manager I respect" ranked #1 over all the other aspects of their work environment including a short commute to work, nice office space or state-of-the-art-technology. Gen Yers said that they want to work with managers who are "pleasant and easy to get along with, understanding and caring, and flexible and open-minded." (Robert Half International, 11) Do not underestimate the importance of your relationship with Generation Y.

Recruiting a New Generation of Teachers

The race to attract qualified teachers becomes more competitive each year. The following tips will help give you an edge in getting more teachers to apply and stay interested during the application process.

Check Out Your District/School Website

Most young adults will investigate and apply for positions online. That is why it is critical to understand how they view the "face" of your school or district online. Does it promote the size of the district and how many people are employed? Some Gen Y teachers are looking for smaller work environments that promote personalization and close working relationships. Your website might be unintentionally sending the wrong message. Young teachers are also very interested in your mentoring program and professional development offered for teachers. They want to know that you will be committed to helping them transition into their chosen profession and support them in continued growth.

Hook Those Prospects and Keep Them Online

Many districts are moving the application process to partially or entirely online. If the process being used is outdated or too cumbersome, you will lose many prospective teachers before they even apply. And after the application is submitted, do you do anything to let them know that they are under consideration? We recommend that someone monitor the list of candidates and send out periodic updates. It is a cost effective way of staying in touch and keeping them on the line. We also suggest that you conduct a survey or focus group with the last cohort of employees to get feedback on their experience; what worked, what didn't. Many businesses conduct customer surveys by mail or telephone to check the level of service and satisfaction. We think that school executives can learn from doing something similar. It will take a small commitment of time, but it will yield a better catch for the next school year.

The School/District Interview, Or Why Should I Teach Here?

Generation Y is also called Generation Why, and they will not be shy about asking pointed questions and why they should teach in your school. Keep in mind that the prospective teaching candidate interview is an opportunity to sell them on your school. Depending on the location and type of certification, they will likely have a number of opportunities available. You want to select the best fit for your school, but the teacher is also reaching a decision about what is best for him or her. We recommend that you involve at least one teacher who is similar in age that you know will have good things to say about the teaching and learning conditions in your school. If you don't know the age before you meet the applicant, have some people on-call who you can introduce to the person during a tour of the school. It is important for new teachers to be able to connect with someone their age and assess their commitment to their school. If you are confident of your staff, it would be ideal to make the introductions and give applicants an opportunity to speak with teachers in small groups in private. By doing so, you communicate trust for your staff and respect for their role in helping support new hires. We have successfully used this technique and recommended it to principals over the years. With some thought and preparation, your staff can help sell your school to the next group of applicants.

What Makes Your School Unique?

We have seen a change in the number and types of questions perspective teachers ask. Teachers coming out of college may be young, but they are not shy about asking why they should select your school over other offers they may have in hand or are considering. You need to be prepared for this question just as you expect the applicant to be ready for your key questions. If you convince them of your commitment to the school and why, they will know what to expect from your leadership. Be ready to explain your school improvement plans and how the staff will work together to reach those objectives. The question will give you a chance to tell the story of what makes your school unique and how you think the applicant can help write the next chapter. Gen Y wants to make a difference in the world, and your school might be the right place for them to start.

How To Get the Most From a Multigenerational Faculty

School executives like the young principal at the beginning of the chapter will need to customize their approach to leading and motivating teachers of a multigenerational faculty. These following recommendations will help guide principals in retaining teachers and reducing the costs associated with staff turnover (Martin & Tulgan, 2006, 146–147).

♦ **Customize staff development.** All schools plan new staff development "opportunities" each year. To create a sense of traction for change in an area of focus, the plan is usually one size fits all. We frequently find that this prescribed training has been dictated by central office for all schools, kindergarten through high school. It is not a bad idea to strive for alignment behind one or two goals, but rarely does the process for improvement apply equally and in the same manner for all teachers. The single professional development model does not work in the classroom, nor does it work for adults. Principals will need to customize the process by gaining input from staff members. The goals may be dictated by outside agencies or in response to student test scores, but the staff should be involved in creating the strategies to meet those goals. Our experience reflects increased buy-in and motivation on the part of teachers at no additional costs. By soliciting ideas from those who have a vested interest in the school's success, the principal may discover untapped expertise and willingness to lead professional development from the ranks of the staff already in the building. By customizing training, principals will maximize the in-house talent of their faculties and ensure that teachers get what they need, regardless of their age or level of experience.

♦ **Control over schedules.** Principals should also be open to customizing work schedules to address the work/life balance of teachers. As they reach retirement, many Baby Boomers would like to have an abbreviated schedule and work part-time. They may be afraid to make that request for a variety of reasons but might be delighted if you let senior members of the staff know that you are open to consideration of that arrangement. The students and staff will benefit from their years of experience and senior teachers will be more accessible to mentor younger teachers. Teachers with 30 plus years are looking forward to a change of pace, but may not be ready for complete withdrawal from the school routine and interactions with students. Part-time work is win-win for teachers and students.

Job sharing is also an attractive alternative for teachers, especially those with small children. The schedules vary, but position sharing accommodates personal needs and keeps strong teachers connected to students and the profession. Principals should also be flexible when it comes to arrival and departure times if they want to hold on to teachers struggling to maintain the work/life balance important to Generation X and Y.

♦ **Control over assignments and location:** In order to retain teachers, especially the novice and alternative route teachers, principals must become
more strategic in the assignment of schedules and location of classrooms.
Two recent studies capture the frustration of teachers just entering their
careers. Susan Moore Johnson and The Project on the Next Generation of
Teachers at the Harvard Graduate School of Education published the project's findings in *Finders and Keepers; Helping New Teachers Survive and Thrive
in Our Schools* (2004). This research reports that:

> teachers were given unusually challenging assignments, which made
> their first years especially difficult. Although schools rarely protected
> new teachers from such assignment, there was no evidence that the
> principal and teachers deliberately tried to make things difficult. Rather,
> these assignments seemed to be the inadvertent consequence of a delayed
> firing process or seniority-based transfer provisions in the teachers'
> contract. When new teachers enter the scene, frequently in late summer
> or early fall, they usually get whatever is left. Although a few principals
> made a deliberate effort to ensure that new teachers' assignments were
> manageable and fair, that was unusual. (p. 104)

Another study titled "Lessons Learned: New Teachers Talk About Their Jobs, Challenges, And Long-Range Plans," conducted by the Public Agenda Foundation's National
Comprehensive Center for Teacher Quality (2008), found that alternative route teachers
are particularly vulnerable to difficult teaching assignments. One new alternative route
teacher put it this way:

> I think that in a lot of other professions, first-year people are mentored and
> eased into it. You start them with easy assignments. I think in education, the
> older teachers have paid their dues, and therefore they teach fewer classes, get
> the honors classes. If you're a first year teacher, you are just muscle almost. I
> know that's what we are here for. (p. 17)

We recommend that principals give a lot of thought and care to the teaching and
room assignment for young teachers. If at all possible, give them a classroom in the
building near their mentor or colleagues who will share materials and strategies and
support them in the early stages of development. Otherwise, you will have to hire a
replacement each year and lose valuable time with students that cannot be recovered.

♦ **Choice of coworkers:** Another way of customizing the workplace is to
allow staff members some choice with whom they work and how often
they meet. Some staff members enjoy collaborating on just about everything, and others prefer to work more independently. Seek input from staff
members before making team or department assignments. Ask them to
describe their approach to working as a member of a team, what they like
to do and what they prefer not to do. Putting teachers on the right position
and team will maximize their strengths and reduce the potential for fric-
tion with their coworkers.

The Perfect Storm

Working with the multigenerational staff can sometimes feel like the "perfect storm." Susan Moore Johnson (2004) describes it this way:

> There is a convergence, then, of several factors that increase the demand for new teachers—massive retirements by veteran teachers, enrollment growth, class-size reductions, the requirement of NCLB, potential teachers' decisions not to pursue a career in teaching, and the attrition and transfer of many new recruits. Together, they create the conditions for a perfect storm in education, a storm in which valuable teaching expertise is lost and never replaced, schools suffer repeated disruption as new teachers come and go, and low-income schools are further undermined by their inability to attract and retain strong teachers. Such a storm might severely weaken the quality of our nation's students. Who will teach, how long they will teach, and how well they will teach depend on choices made today. (p. 15)

An awareness of the characteristics of each generation in the teaching force, their unique needs, and how to lead the multigenerational faculty will help you make the right choices beginning today.

7

Leading High Performance Teams

Have you ever been a part of a high performing team? We've both been fortunate to be a part of high performing teams; one in starting up a new school, and the other in designing professional development for school principals on a statewide rollout. These hardworking teams are focused on success, and they have an easy rapport among the members. You may have been privileged to have been a part of a high performing team. Contrast the characteristics of high performing teams with those situations where the word "team" is used in derision. You may have been part of one of these working groups:

♦ The "bland leading the bland" where there is no inspiration, sense of urgency or excitement

♦ A "social club," where members enjoy each other's company, but there is little accountability for results

♦ A "sniper alley," where each new idea is shot down and members look for cover each time an innovative idea surfaces

Here are practical, battle-tested strategies that can help you improve your team's performance, whether you are a formal leader or a team member.

Developing the Team

A generally accepted definition of a team is a relatively small number of people who come together and who:

1. share common goals

2. share the responsibility and accountability for meeting those goals

3. set aside their own individual goals for the overriding goals of those common goals

Define Your Team

It's perfectly acceptable to recognize that you may not have a team under these criteria. A team is not a workgroup. A team is not simply a collection of people who report to a common manager or executive. A team should not be a group of people who share ideas but have stronger goals for which they are individually responsible. For example, you may have:

- ◆ different grade level or department level groups that call themselves teams
- ◆ a school leadership "team," comprised of grade level chairs, your assistant principal(s), and your lead secretary
- ◆ a school improvement "team," where you have parents, community members, faculty members, and staff representatives
- ◆ a general board for a nonprofit community service organization

You need to define what you want this group to accomplish. Will this group come together quickly and then disband after the short-term assignment, or will this team stay together for a long period of time?

Is there a process for a "changing of the guard" that will result in a periodic rotation of members? Many standing organizations have specific rotation policies where individuals have a specified term and then must step down for a period of time.

Beware of Barriers That Destroy Teams

There are several barriers that can destroy or significantly impede people's impact on creating and defining a team.

Inbred Teams. You will likely get results of the lowest common denominator from your group when it consists of people who have similar backgrounds and perspectives within the same organization. For example, if your goal is to improve performance of students in minority subgroups, the team members must represent those subgroups on which you hope to have an impact. According to Scott Page (2008), diverse perspectives enable teams to find more and better solutions and contribute to overall productivity. Page cautions that coming to a decision via a diverse group is harder and takes more time.

Let's take an example of trying to increase parent participation in school activities.

You serve in a school that has many working class families on shift work or who work two and sometimes three jobs to make ends meet. You have been concerned that the back-to-school night activities, parent-teacher conferences, or student performances have consistent low turnout. If you convene a group to come up with solutions to this problem, you may inadvertently include teachers and parents who have long-standing involvement or have been active parent volunteers. If you don't intentionally create diversity of thought by including some parents who have *not* been actively involved but you know want to participate, you fall prey to the inbred behavior that got you in this predicament in the first place.

You have to listen and act on the perspectives of people you are trying to win over, even when it is uncomfortable. If one of the action steps to increase inclusion is to go to community centers and have parent meetings at that location, you have to go and take a group of teachers with you. Meeting with families in the evening where they live may be a new experience for some of your teachers as well as parents. They haven't done it before and it is out of their comfort zone. To help overcome this dilemma, you should find ways to bring people in to give their perspective and help teachers and staff work more effectively with these subgroups. Teachers that understand the cultural differences can discuss what might be of importance to these families and how to approach difficult issues. If no teachers have the necessary background, you could invite a community leader or social worker to meet with the team to provide further context.

Losing Faith. Losing faith may be defined as a lack of confidence among team members in their peer's intentions. When you have a work group that has lost faith, they end up sniping with each other and questioning the motives of other team members. Ultimately they focus their time and energy on what others say and do, not the purpose of the work. When we worked with a struggling school's school improvement team, we were disturbed by the amount of critiquing, questioning the motives of various team members suggestions for improvement, and the subtle hostility that periodically boiled over in numerous sidebar discussions that focused more on personalities rather than the work and issues that needed to be discussed.

You have been in work groups where people say exactly what the manager wants them to say during the meeting. After the meeting adjourns, cliques and small groups of two and three congregate in different areas analyzing, critiquing, and questioning the outcomes of the meeting. One group we worked with called these informal clique critiques "the meeting after the meeting." How much energy is wasted analyzing the motivation, the politicking, and the sniping within these "meetings after the meetings"?

Lack of Conflict. Not all conflict is bad. In fact, conflict is frequently very useful in getting to the root cause of a problem, or understanding different perspectives that can help the team reach the best decisions. The late Peter Drucker called it "disagreeing without being disagreeable," (2006). Many teams go through a fairly predictable sequence in dealing with conflict. First, people must trust each other and value different perspectives. Members of the group must believe that others are advocating for the right cause without trying to advance themselves. If trust does not exist, then individuals are typically reluctant to challenge each other's assumptions and assertions. Then your role as a leader is to try to draw out and challenge these assumptions, asking questions like "What data supports what you are saying?," or "Walk us through how you came to that conclusion." You must be prepared to draw out conflict and differing points of view from each member. It is wise to challenge previously held assumptions and have group members challenge you as well. Yet, set the expectation that you want people to challenge each other's assumptions without resorting to sarcasm, belittling, or attacking the person. Finally, you want to clarify how you plan for the decision to be made.

Effective teams fight frequently and often. What separates effective teams from ineffective teams is the way that they fight. Effective teams fight about the issues. During meetings, (especially if you have taken care to bring diverse points of view into the team), people will voice differing points of view, opinions, and perspectives. When this happens, meetings are passionate, intense, compelling and vital. People question each other's assumptions, challenge statements that are not based upon facts, and are comfortable enough to speak up. The leader's role in this type of highly productive meeting is to ensure that:

- ◆ everybody's voice is heard

- ◆ assumptions are questioned and challenged in a way that focuses upon the issue, not the person

- ◆ group norms of fairness, integrity, and dignity are preserved in these meetings

At the end of the meeting, people should be able to say that they had a chance to voice their opinions, concerns, proposals, and suggestions. It does *not* mean that the decision made has to be one of consensus, which can (though not always) lead to the lowest common denominator among the team members.

Setting Expectations—Get a GRIP

To ensure the success of a team, you must be clear about the goals you want your team to accomplish, how they will accomplish it, and by when and how you will measure their results. One effective acronym you can use to think through these expectations is the acronym GRIP, which stands for Goals, Responsibilities, Interpersonal expectations, and Processes. We'll use a district-level middle school report card committee to illustrate each of these concepts and how an effective leader can use the approach to get better results from her team.

The committee is comprised of a cross-section of principals, teachers, parents, and central office executives. The leader is the assistant superintendent for curriculum and instruction. The district's policy is to review and make recommendations every 5 years for changes to the middle school report card based upon current research and other district policies.

Let's see how GRIP can be applied to their task.

Goals

You must know up front what you want to accomplish, what resources are available, the measure by which you will know success, and when the goal has to be accomplished. In the report card committee, the assistant superintendent did a fair amount of preparation. She knew:

- ◆ what needed to be accomplished (a review and recommendations to the school board for any changes in the middle school report card)

- ◆ when it had to be done (within 90 days)

- ◆ which groups had to have input (parents, teachers, principals)

- ◆ how she was going to measure success (recommendations approved by the board with input from various factions)

The assistant superintendent laid out the charter for the group at the first meeting. She explained that members of the committee were selected because of their diverse skills, perspectives, and backgrounds. She also laid out the timeline and her requirements for success. She made clear that at the end of each meeting each representative would go back to their stakeholders with an update. The representative was asked to take a pulse of what was being discussed and get feedback on the recommendations.

Responsibilities

As the team leader, you must clarify the roles and responsibilities for each group member. This idea (organizational clarity) gives a sense of alignment: people, money, and time are positioned around common goals. This alignment creates focus and autonomy. Everybody knows their individual responsibility and other individuals' responsibility. The positive effect is that people don't waste time trying to figure out who has to complete each task and that multiple people are not working redundantly on the same problem or issue and getting "out of their swim lanes." Consider who may possess the necessary technical and interpersonal skills and strengths before assigning roles and responsibilities. To help you reach the best decision, remember to keep diversity of opinion in mind. This is another example of "getting the right people on the bus in the right seats (Collins, 2005). Help your team accomplish their goals by interpreting *what* has to be accomplished, the parameters, the performance standards, and the timeline

The assistant superintendent skillfully handled this part of the GRIP when she outlined why she chose each person on the team, what skills each person brought, and what she expected out of each person (actively contribute, report back to stakeholders, and come up with recommendations).

Interpersonal Expectations

You have to set your expectations for team members in terms of their interpersonal interactions with each other and within the team. Common expectations include attendance to meetings, eliminating interruptions from cell phones, discouraging sidebar conversations, and speaking up versus not participating in the discussion. The leader should encourage vigorous discussion around issues while maintaining dignity for the opinion and perspective of the person (even though there will be disagreements based upon those different perspectives). Another expectation may be that each representative must report out to and back from subgroups.

The assistant superintendent laid out her expectations during the first meeting: what skills and strengths that each person had to contribute to the team and what she expected from each team member. She emphasized that she expected each person to speak up and to challenge each other's assumptions. She stated her belief that silence indicates assent. She encouraged members to make recommendations based upon facts and upon the best interests of the students and parents, rather than administrative or teacher convenience. She also made explicit that once the decision is made, there should be no second-guessing and backstabbing from group participants.

Processes

As a leader, you are responsible for setting the parameters for the goal. You are also responsible for helping people understand how accomplishing the goal fits into the larger context of the district's and superintendent's plans. If you bring a group of people together and make the assumption that everybody knows why they are together as a team, then you may well have people working at cross purposes to each other. In setting parameters for the team, you should focus on both what has to be accomplished and what success looks like. You should be able to give your team the parameters in responses to questions like:

- When we are successful, what will be different from what is happening today?
- What difference will accomplishing this challenge make?
- What are the measurements (metrics) that will help us to measure success?
- What are the milestones, deliverables, and deadlines for accomplishing this challenge?
- What is out-of-bounds for us?

The assistant superintendent stressed the importance of communicating back to stakeholders and active involvement. She also stressed that each team member had the obligation to share all suggestions, fact-based critiques, or a perspectives with the group. She also outlined the decision making process and explained that task force recommendations would go to the superintendent. The superintendent had the responsibility to share the recommendations with the board of education, and that the board of education had the final decision making authority.

As a result of the assistant superintendent using this framework, she was able to help the district meet its policy mandate to review and revise the middle school report card with reduced anxiety and pushback from different constituent groups. The superintendent took the committee's recommendation to the board, which made some minor modifications based upon additional feedback from the community forums. One board member noted that this round of report card revisions was one of the smoothest reviews in his memory.

Other Leadership Tasks and Tactics

Here are some other considerations for developing and deploying a high performance team.

Use A Hook

A key task for you as the team leader is to quickly set the stage for why the team has been assembled, outline the challenge, and the importance of meeting the challenge. Many effective school executives use a "hook" to link the goal accomplishment to larger goals. Think for a moment about a favorite fiction writer, a TV show, or your favorite movie. These three illustrations share a common trait. They find a way to hook us within the first 5 pages or 5 minutes of the story. You can use the method that great writers use to communicate the challenge and parameters.

An example of using a hook comes from a principal and her annual back-to-school faculty meeting. The principal (Barb) set the challenge for her faculty and staff. Barb's school achievement for the previous year was flat. The school had a persistent problem of not meeting the goals for children on free or reduced lunch. Barb's back-to-school faculty meetings were generally heavy on the administrative aspect of opening school. In the past, she used PowerPoint slides with lots of bar graphs and line charts that looked like spaghetti.

This time Barb wanted to turn the statistics into a story. At the opening staff meeting, she first asked the faculty to talk in table groups about why they chose to be teachers or to work in a support role in a school. After reporting back to the entire group, Barb flashed a couple of charts on the screen, sharing statistics as she had done before. Next, she projected a collage of 25 grayed out pictures of individual students on the screen, ensuring that the pictures had no identifying characteristics of any students. She pointed out that 10 of those 25 students (40%) were not achieving up to their potential. Finally, she showed a picture of a homeroom from the previous year, ending with "We all came into this job for similar reasons. Earlier this morning you spoke about what motivated you to become an educator. At the end of the year, let's make sure that we can tell the parents of these students how proud we are of their children's progress. Your challenge is to create unit and lesson plans that help each child grow and achieve this year better than they have ever done before."

Focus on The "What," Not The "How"

In a story recounted by Scott Eblin (2006), a former chief operating officer, Bob Pittman reminded his colleagues that as leaders, they were "the keepers of the *what*, not the masters of the *how*." Knowing the right answer is not the most important thing. If you call a team together, you have to allow them to determine the best way to proceed and achieve the goal within the parameters you have set. You add the most value as a team leader by facilitating the team and interpreting the work of others and its impact on the goals, not by determining the one best way to accomplish the goal.

Facilitate

As a school executive, you have access to additional knowledge, information, and perspectives. Your team members generally have greater knowledge of their individual areas of expertise. Communicate facts, information, and impressions as a way of helping the team understand its goals, parameters, and constraints. Sharing information will provide a stronger connection to you and a deeper understanding of your plans for the school and the importance of their work.

Another way that you facilitate the team is by using your influence to secure additional resources or to knock down barriers so that your team can get their goal accomplished. Every organization has its bureaucratic silos and culture. If your team needs additional information, the person who has that information will likely share it more readily when requested by you (one school executive to another) than in response to a request from a teacher. Your role here is to provide resources to your team and remove as many road-blocks as possible to help them get what they need from the school and district.

Interpret

Your role is to ensure that the work is accurate and completed on time. You must also frame the broader implications of what your team is doing to the larger organization. You cannot and should not dig into all of the details of the work. During the plans and process stages (GRIP), you helped your team create performance standards and bench-marks. Careful monitoring of their work will allow you to move to the final stage of framing the implications of their work to the organization and community. Faculty and staff might have a limited view and perspective since they are so focused on teaching children. Staff members interact with each other, with their neighborhood, social friends and church members, and with the parents of the children they teach. At principals' meetings, district and community meetings, you learn about the current burning issues and how other schools are handling certain challenges. Nobody but you has this oppor-tunity, insight, and perspective, which are highly valuable to shape direction and to drive action through your team (Eblin, 2006). Sharing your perspective helps your team determine the "Why" behind the "What" that you have outlined for them, so they can do a better job of the "How" to accomplish the tasks.

Develop Talent

As an executive developing a team, be aware also of developing individuals. Your team members can benefit from this opportunity to grow and stretch beyond their current set of skills and talents. They gain experience and exposure to think and act in fresh ways, which can easily lead to gaining additional insights, and in turn, take even more responsibility—which leverages your time. Therefore, be careful to remember the differ-ence between "stretchwork and fetchwork" (Townsend, 1995). There are certainly tasks that have to be done and delegated to other people. Use your work with teams to help develop people's talent, give them different perspectives, and help them to think beyond their current functional areas.

Set Up Communication Systems

As you deploy your team, you should set up systems to communicate what is going on in the school. You likely already send out summary e-mails or have team leads send out status e-mails on what is going on with different initiatives. You also update your various stakeholders through newsletters and flyers. We've seen school executives use blogs, discussion board forums, and wikis to update people on the status of different initiatives. They use these tools to cut down on e-mail traffic by referring people to the running threads in the discussion board, blog, or wiki. To find out more about blogs, wikis, discussion boards, and other Web 2.0 technologies, talk with your district IT expert or check out the Landmarks for Schools website at www.landmark-project.com for additional information.

Using Questions

Skillful school executives share their perspectives, experience, and insight in several different ways. One of the best ways is to ask effective questions. Effective questions have several different characteristics:

♦ Questions start open ended.

♦ Questions provide exposure to different perspectives.

♦ Questions force listeners to think through the implications of different options.

♦ Questions take more time initially but take less time in subsequent meetings.

One of the best leadership teachers we learned from is a gentleman named Jack McCall. Jack is a master of the Socratic method. He reminded us several times that people are not "nonrational." Rather, logic, facts, and figures only go so far. When we rely solely upon logic and data, we assume that others will automatically buy in to our plan. It almost never happens that way. Jack taught us that simply using statements and commands invites only tacit agreement or submission. Effective use of questions, on the other hand, engages people, helps your team to understand your viewpoint, leads them to create their own logic and conclusions, and helps them to think through other possibilities that can help them better get to the "how" more effectively. Stever Robbins (2004) suggests that when you design your questions first map out the logic that leads to your conclusions and then use "how" and "why" questions.

"How" questions, according to Robbins, help people move from high level goals to specifics. When you ask "how questions," you can align district level goals all the way down to individual level. In fact, when you take your own goals and ask "How can we reach these?," you can take those answers to create goals for your team and individuals.

"Why" questions, on the other hand, go from specifics to overall reasons. Asking your custodian "why" questions might result in the follow exchange.

Q: "Why are you cleaning the classroom?"

A: "Because kids need clean classrooms."

Q: "Why do the students need clean classrooms?"

A: "The students and teachers can concentrate on learning, rather than taking out the trash and sweeping the class."

Q: "Why do they need to concentrate on learning?"

A: "To achieve their learning goals, and the school can achieve its learning goals."

"Why questions" allow you to better align your individual activities with the school's overall mission, vision, and goals.

You may have been part of a high performing team. The feeling of interdependence, focus, and trust combined with accomplishment of the goal and mission is very satisfying. We hope these tactics and strategies for building, developing, and deploying high performing teams will help you "crack the code" and consistently build these high performing teams.

8

Making Sure Your School Improvement Plan Works

It's been a tough year for you and your school. You've seen a steady decline in your school's test scores. You've noticed that for the past 3 years, your students' achievement for those who have English as a Second Language (ESL) has been flat. It's been that way even though you've exhorted teachers to focus on these students to help them achieve more. In addition, your highest achieving students have suffered from "achievement flat lining." The only growth has been with students who qualify for free and reduced lunch and those children who are, as one teacher noted "just good plain kids." The fact that over 20% of your teachers can retire at the end of this year is also of concern. Fully half of those teachers are in critical teaching areas. This data creates a potential issue in terms of staffing for the upcoming year. It also creates a potential source of anxiety for your PTSA and other community members. As you prepare to log off your computer for the week, you receive a high priority e-mail from the superintendent's executive assistant. The superintendent wants you to present your annual school improvement plan to the superintendent's cabinet and the board of education in 2 weeks. You sigh, record the due date on your calendar, create a task item, insert it in your 43 file folders, and set an appointment with yourself to start working on this next week.

What Is a Strong School Improvement Process?

School improvement planning sounds like a dull and arduous task reserved only for those at the highest levels. The essence of school improvement planning is determining what you *are* going to do and what you *are not* going to do. Strong school improvement planning begins with thinking through what you see happening on the inside and outside of the school and then determining how the school will respond. There are two myths that we encounter in our work with school executives who are engaging in school improvement planning and implementation.

1. **Myth**: Some people think that school improvement planning is something that you do along a timeline, usually in the summer, and then unveil it to others at the start of the school year.

   Reality: School improvement planning is not a linear process. It is a continuous course of action. The following 4-step process is adapted from Donald Sull (2007).

   ♦ Try something (making sense).

   ♦ Make choices (determining your priorities and allocating resources to those priorities).

   ♦ Make it happen (implementing what you say you are going to do and by what dates).

   ♦ Make adjustments (looking at the performance metrics that you have established; then decide what is going well and what is not going well and make mid-year corrections).

This 4-step cycle can be done quarterly and annually and should be maintained while the plan is in effect.

2. **Myth:** Many people confuse a school improvement plan with a mission statement, district values, and/or a vision statement.

   Reality: Mission statements basically tell the world why we exist. These mission statements often have a phrase like "to help all children (students) achieve their highest potential," to "empower teachers and community members," and " to be considered a premier school (or district) in the district (or state)." Avoid confusing your mission (why your school exists) and vision (what you want to be) with strategy (what specific actions will your school take to achieve your mission and vision; Raisel & Friga, 2001).

This route to school improvement planning provides multiple opportunities to incorporate current data and translate that new information into action. Those who view the document as written on stone tablets will have difficulty motivating the staff to get behind the plan and implement the components reflected in the staff development and training portion of the plan.

Making Sense

The first step is to determine what you want to achieve. Try this exercise first alone and then with your school improvement team. The first question requires you to consider target goals for student achievement and how to build the faculty's capacity to meet those goals.

What do we want our school to have accomplished at the end of 2 years?

You will also need to examine your personal development and identify the areas where you will need to stretch and grow as well. You may also want to ask, "What do we want as our end result?," or "What do we want to be known for?" This analysis should include staff and community members. You will likely have vigorous and spirited discussions. Your role in these discussions is to serve as the conscience of the students who don't have anybody to speak for them.

Your fact base can illuminate possible patterns and trends (see chapter 4, "Resource Management"). You have to have a large enough body of facts, trends, and patterns to create a larger picture that includes alternative views and solutions, rather than lasering in on the first viewpoint that you think is viable.

Making Choices

Your second question is

How will we prioritize these results?

Focus your organizational resources and attention on a small number of clear priorities. Drucker (2006) noted that many executives in nonprofit organizations have difficulty having too many priorities for precious few resources. As a result, they spread themselves too thin and have trouble achieving *any* of their priorities. Late in life, Drucker spent the vast majority of his time consulting with nonprofit and social service agencies. He was famous for responding to the plea of nonprofit executives that "we have so many needs—we can't eliminate any of them. . . . In fact we need more money because of all of these needs." Drucker's paraphrased response was that there are indeed so many needs and those needs are growing. At the same time, we have a precious finite number of resources—people, money, time and space. He asked what is it that we can do with these precious few resources so that we can see the most impact. Many management and leadership experts strongly suggest that you should have three to five priorities, three being preferable. Distilling your priorities to three major areas serves to clarify, focus, and compel people to action.

After you have distilled three to five priorities, the next question is

Which resources (time, money, space, and people)
will we allocate to each priority?

You will likely have another spirited and passionate discussion with this conversation, hearing comments like:

"We can't do anything about this!"

"We have such a limited budget right now and need grant money to do what we want to do!"

"What do we tell people who we are no longer able to help?"

"How do we respond to the community?"

One of the hard parts of being a principal is being able to find ways that you can be more efficient with your current resources to reallocate those "found" dollars to go toward your new initiative. You might ask how young teachers decide to put money aside to buy their first house. Even with the relatively small salaries that teachers make, many young teachers make home ownership a priority and set aside money in their monthly budget to save enough for a down payment for their first home.

School executives may be surprised by the creativity and collaboration that takes place when a careful allocation of resources is implemented. We saw one elementary school's grade level reduce their paper usage by 40% by having teachers use small chalkboards and chalk rather than using handouts for math practice. They were able to reallocate that money for computer software to help the students practice higher level thinking skills with simulation software.

Once you have gone through the "making sense" and "making choices" steps, next examine the strengths and weaknesses of the school. Changes in priorities and resource allocation must be aligned between external accountability and current conditions inside the school. Otherwise, teachers may say, "This is what we have, and this is what we can do. If the two don't match, we're sorry but we cannot do anything about it."

Examine Strengths and Weaknesses

You want to think through your school's strengths and what areas that you consider a weakness, a challenge, or an area of concern. One approach is to take each of the top three priorities you identified earlier during your external analysis. Create a table by recording each priority in a column across the top and add three rows below. Determine whether the priority is a strength now, could be a strength in the near term, or is currently a weakness (see Figure 8.1).

Analyze Your Faculty

Earlier we identified three major priorities as an example: low ESL achievement, low achievement by high performing students, and lack of technology usage to differentiate instruction. Say that after a review of data, you found that there is an increased number of children who need remediation to get up to grade level as well as accelerated learning for children who are academically gifted or very high performing. You also understand that there will be no increases to your budget to support new instructional initiatives. Assume that your district has a priority to increase the use of technology as a tool to differentiate and accelerate learning. You can then analyze your faculty's strengths and weaknesses in these areas. Consider each faculty member and ask: "Where do I see this person in each of these three priorities?"

1. *"Can this teacher consistently provide remediation for children who have English as a Second Language (ESL)?"*

2. *"Can this teacher accelerate learning for high achieving students?"*

3. *"What is their skill in using technology as a learning tool to differentiate instruction?"*

Finally, insert the last names in each of the three cells as in the example below. You can also bold the names of those teachers ready to retire within 3 years. The completed table (Figure 8.1) will provide a tool for customizing professional development based upon individual strengths and weaknesses of your faculty.

FIGURE 8.1 Specific Strengths and Needs Worksheet

	Accelerating learning for ESL subgroup	**Accelerating learning for high achievers**	**Using technology to differentiate instruction**
Currently a strength	**Patterson**	**Cannon**	Lynn **Cannon**
Could be a strength in the short-term	Lynn Watkins	Williams **Patterson**	Watkins Smith **Patterson** Buxton
Weakness	**Cannon** Smith Williams Buxton	Watkins Lynn Buxton Smith	Williams

Analyze Your School—The McKinsey 7-S Model

One of the most respected and long running management consulting companies, the McKinsey Corporation, developed a model to analyze organizations and to consider the fit between different aspects of the organization. This model, called the 7-S model, looked at the following areas: structure, skills, shared values, staff, systems, style, and strategy. The following questions will help you determine if the area is a strength, a weakness, or neutral.

- ♦ **Structure**: How is your school structured? For example, how are the grade levels or departments organized? Do you have departmentalized or integrated classrooms? How are students placed in classes? How do you determine which teachers teach which classes? How are faculty/grade level/department meetings conducted?

- ♦ **Skills**: What skills do you, the leadership team, and the faculty have? Are those skills the ones necessary to successfully respond to the issues outlined in your external analysis? Do you have a skill gap in any those areas? This is where the strengths and weaknesses chart above can help you identify skill gaps.

- ♦ **Shared Values**: What are the ways that your school celebrates successes? How do you orient your new teachers? How do you orient new students and parents? How do you communicate important news? What is the relationship between the parent teacher organization, external stakeholders, and the school? What are the informal behaviors that shape your school? This is the area that most school executives call "culture."

♦ **Staff**: How do you hire staff? What are the skills that you look for? How do you involve your teachers in staff selection? What are their particular strengths?

♦ **Systems**: What systems do you have in place to monitor what is going on in your school? How do you keep track of what funds have been actually spent on your strategic priorities? How do you monitor instruction with your observation schedule? What types of data do you collect and share with teachers? How do you monitor discipline issues? How do you track and monitor key assignments that you have delegated to other people?

♦ **Style**: What is your management and decision-making style?

♦ **Strategy**: All of these areas then tie into your strategy, much like a spider web.

Making It Happen

After you and your leadership team have decided on which priorities to focus, you need to decide how you will accomplish your goals.

Questions To Answer Upfront

You'll reap the benefits of solid planning when you start by answering questions like:

♦ What specific activities will we, our leadership team, our teachers, and our community do?

♦ What resources will be allocated to these activities?

♦ Who is accountable to complete each of these activities?

♦ What performance measures will we use to gauge success?

♦ What is the timeline to complete each of these activities?

♦ Will we do these alone or are we going to engage in alliances or partnerships to complete the activities?

Once you have made your choices, you need to determine who is going to do what by what date, with what resources, and with what performance measures. Let's look at each of these in turn:

Who is going to do *What*? By *What Date*? With *What Resources*? Everybody is busy and has more than they can do. Nonetheless, if you are going to accomplish what you have outlined, you need to have a single point of contact for each part or subpart of your plan. That is the person that you are going to go to for updates and status reports.

What are the *Performance Measures*? How will you know whether you are on track, off track, succeeding or not succeeding?

Performance Measures

There are some key points in setting performance measures.

No single measure will accurately capture all you are trying to achieve. In addition, each measure has unintended side effects. One example of the unintended side effects of metrics occurred when one district mandated that principals had to complete and report in 15 "walk-through observations" per week. The district got exactly what they were measuring—the number of walk-throughs, but not what the principals were supposed to be looking for or any tangible evidence of what the principals actually saw during the walk-through. The district leadership and principals quickly adapted their initial requirement and created additional metrics for the walk-throughs.

You'll never be able to find one magic measurement which captures all of what you are trying to measure. Focus on a small number (3-5) of metrics that give provide a good data picture. If you have more than 5 measures, you spend more time reporting on the metrics than actually doing the work. If your team doesn't see the value in the metric, you will end up getting derailed.

Don't measure something if you cannot act upon the results. By the same token, don't take the easy way out by using some measures "just because we can get that data easily."

Managing Initiatives

Two popular different ways to approach and manage your initiative on one sheet of paper or the linear approach (see Figure 8.2 on page 114) and the fishbone diagram (see Figure 8.4 on page 116).

1. Using the linear approach, you first determine what you want to accomplish by the end of the year. Then work backwards and ask: What has to be accomplished at the 12-month mark? To accomplish the results by then, who has to do what and by when? You then work backward from the 12-month mark to the 6-month mark, to the 3-month mark and so on. (see Figures 8.2 and 8.3)

2. The second method is adapted from a major technology company that has grown through acquiring other companies. Their acquisition team uses a fishbone diagram to capture what they expect to accomplish and how to measure it. The team completed a fishbone diagram for every 3-month period beginning with the final goal and working back to the current conditions. They then ask, "to accomplish this 1-month milestone with this metric, what do we need to do, who is responsible for it (initials in parentheses), by what date and with what budget (in $). They insert their data in the lines below the main horizontal line. They then continue moving counterclockwise to each succeeding diagonal slashmark above the horizontal line going through the same set of questions. (see Figure 8.4)

FIGURE 8.2 Sample: Making it Happen

Goal	Outcome	Completion Date
Meet Annual Yearly Progress (AYP)	All six subgroups in school will meet AYP based on state mandated tests	May 20, 20--

12 month plan

Objectives	Who	By When
Administer Annual End of Year Exams	All	5/15
Final Test Prep	Teachers	5/1

6 months

Objectives	Who	By When
Quarterly review of action strategies/revisions	Principal/Teachers/ Assistant Principal	2/22
Analyze benchmark test results	Teachers	2/10
Administer benchmark tests	Teachers	2/1

3 months

Objectives	Who	By When
Quarterly review of action strategies success/revision	Principal/Teachers/ Assistant Principal	10/20
Analyze benchmark results	Teachers	10/10
Administer benchmark tests	Teachers	10/5

1 month

Objectives	Who	By When
Set up new strategy: first 15 minutes of faculty meetings to focus on action items/strategies that work w/different subgroups	Principal	9/1
Action Items/Strategies from teachers	Grade Chairs	9/1

2 weeks

Objectives	Who	By When
Review analysis with Assistant Principals	Principal	8/3
Complete grade level meetings w/strategies/action items for teachers to meet targets	Principal	8/3
Complete first level analysis for different courses by subgroups using Pivot Tables	Principal	8/1

1 week

Objectives	Who	By When
Receive test data data in soft copy	Test Coordinator	7/28
Print out goal summary reports by grade level for each teacher in upcoming classes	Secretary	7/28

Within 24 Hours

Objectives	Who	By When
Call Test Coordinator for test data in soft copy	Principal	

FIGURE 8.3   Sample: Making it Happen

Goal	Outcome	Completion Date

12 month plan

Objectives	Who	By When

6 months

3 months

1 month

2 weeks

1 week

Within 24 Hours

FIGURE **8.4** Fishbone Diagram

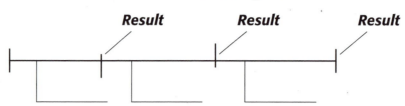

Making Adjustments

In making adjustments, it is important to communicate to your stakeholders that the priorities, choices, timelines, and measures are the team's best guess at the time. Remind your stakeholders that circumstances may change based upon new information. You should collect and analyze real-time data similar to the process that researchers use in scientific experiments. Examine what has happened, use the resulting facts to confirm or revise your assumptions, priorities, and implementation plans. Your fundamental role in these discussions is what Sull calls "intellectual humility . . . which is not the most common attribute among executives" (2007). You need to exemplify and set the stage by adopting a stance of inquiry, not advocacy. In theory, this should be simple.

♦ You convene the team to discuss what they expected to happen and why (what facts supported what was expected to happen).

♦ You compare what they expected to what actually happened.

♦ You explore the gaps between expectations and reality.

UNC professors Alism Frasale, Paul Frige, and Dave Hofmann outline some common blindspots in decision making and strategy. We've adapted their lessons to school improvement planning.

Mitigating the Risks of Blind Spots

As you develop your strategy to support various initiatives with your team, you should be aware of possible problems (see Figure 8.5).

FIGURE 8.5   Blind Spots and Possible Solutions

Problem	Possible Solution
Continuing To Invest in a Bad Decision: People tend to like to win and be perceived as winners. You are guilty of this when you continue to pour resources (time, money, and people) into a program even when you have evidence that the current course of action is not getting the intended results. For example, you invest in a reading program that is supposed to show great gains for students. You have trained people in this program, and you've implemented it faithfully for the past 2 years. You then find that you are not getting the gains that you hoped for. It is now time to "recertify" for this program. You are guilty of throwing bad money after good if you decide that "Well, we've already invested all of this money and time—we may as well go ahead and recertify."	The best antidote for this problem is outlining specific results you expect from this program, by when, and what additional resources will be allocated to the initiative. You are essentially engaging in a portfolio of mini-experiments. The idea of a "pilot" or "proof of concept" is a good way to try to get a small win without putting all of your resources in a make-or-break plan. As with any experiment, you want to know what you expect to find at its conclusion. You can expand the experiment if it works. If it doesn't work as well as you had hoped (by setting up clear performance metrics upfront), then you can cut your losses, move on, and try another strategy.
Limited Point of View: You are limited to accurately assess what is possible due to your limited frame of reference. If you have ever heard a teacher say "We've always done it this way. It has worked fine. Why do we need to look at another way of doing this?," this person is guilty of the limited frame of reference.	This most often occurs when principals get stale or lose our thirst for learning and expanding our horizons. Expanding horizons can come from workshops, conferences, seminars, or professional journals.
Invalid Assumptions: You make "myth based assumptions" (boys are better than girls in math and science) or form unchallenged theories of what is going on based upon outdated information.	Make your assumptions explicit and based on your data. Require people to challenge the assumptions that you are making. If others have different assumptions that are based on fact, then add them to the stew.
"N=1": You hear a generalization based upon a very small, nonrandom, or unrepresentative sample. You see this frequently when an organization makes a shift based on what one individual overheard.	Beware of the small sample size factor. Examine the validity of the evidence before making assumptions and decisions.
Self-interest: This occurs when one's parochial self-interests overcome the interests of the organization as a whole. You may find this when an individual wants to "win recognition" in order to stoke his or her competitive fires, build a resume, or be seen as a "creative, innovative, and decisive leader."	Awareness is the best antidote for this blind spot. Look in the mirror and ensure that you are doing making the deal for the right reasons—to help children and to help teachers help children. The right reasons can also include a positive side effect of being able to publicize your efforts publicly.

Continued

Figure 8.5 Blind Spots and Possible Solutions

Problem	Possible Solution
Problem Framing: This refers to inability to think through the issue from various viewpoints before diving right into a solution. For example, a school executive wants to get the problem resolved quickly and then move on to other issues. This rapid problem -solving rational model works with easily identified and small-stakes problems. It is folly to use this rapid decision-making model on strategic issues.	Take the time to think through the problem from different perspectives. What does this problem look like from the points of view of the community, central office, teachers, staff, superintendent, and any other stakeholders. Do they see the problem in the same way that you do? If not, what does their perspective share?
"Everything's Great" Bias: We all have a tendency to share only the good news with our superintendent, the school board, and the community. Consistently sharing good news is a savvy community relations tool. Yet, if you are consistently sharing only the good news, these same people that you are trying to influence may be increasingly skeptical and think that you are simply trying to "sell them a bill of goods."	We could simply say "be authentic and truthful, " but there is more. One tactic that we've learned from work with senior leaders is the concept of "send bad news quickly, summarize, and share good news periodically." Whenever there is a "bad news" issue, quickly communicate that to your manager, along with what you are doing to solve the problem. As one senior leader shared, "bad news is not like wine. It doesn't get better with age." Each month, send a one-page summary of the "good news and activities" of the past month to your manager and superintendent.

That's a Great Question

You've used the models and tools in this chapter to outline your top three pressing school improvement issues. You've worked with your school improvement team to filter down the top two or three issues that your school will focus upon. You've analyzed the strengths and weaknesses of the staff and school. You've outlined a prioritized school improvement plan with metrics, resources, and timelines.

At the monthly school board meeting, you make your way to the front row. Midway through the meeting, you are called up to address the board. Immediately, a school board member says, "We've noticed that your school achievement hasn't done as well as we all hoped. What do you see as the main issue and what suggestions do you have for improving your school?" You smile inwardly and answer, "That's a great question. While we're not satisfied with our performance, we've done some significant analysis and would like to share our findings with you along with what we think has the greatest potential for improving our school during the next year."

9

Decision-Making Disabilities and How To Avoid Them

Imagine that during a recent leadership meeting, you outlined a process you thought was the equivalent to casting a small pebble in a pond. Instead, the process created a tsunami of discontent among your faculty, staff, and parents. The new process seemed simple enough. After three near misses with a carpooler and faculty vehicles, you adjusted the location of the carpool lanes and bus lines and eliminated a left turn out of the parking lot to get your students and teachers out more quickly and safely. Simple, right? The results have been snide comments muttered in the hallways, parents calling the superintendent's office, and a lack of support from the district transportation department. Now everybody's lobbying for a return to the old way of school dismissal that is putting your entire schools' leadership team into a destructive spiral of discontent.

School executives consider themselves to be fairly rational people. We try to go through a rational decision-making model:

- ♦ clearly identify the problem

- ♦ identify what we want to accomplish

- ♦ identify options

- ♦ evaluate those options

- ♦ select the option that gives us our best chance to achieve what we want to accomplish

This rational decision making model works pretty well most of the time (Simon, 1997). Yet, we are all are afflicted with various strange workings of our nonrational minds. These strange workings, or "management decision-making disabilities," cannot

119

be totally eliminated. In fact, many times we don't use the rational decision-making model in its entirety. Herbert Simon, a Nobel Prize winner, coined the term *satisficing*, meaning a decision that is good enough. Satisficing makes tradeoffs among our need to be right, to be seen as an expert, time pressures, and our personal decision-making style. Our needs compete with other's needs, including group norms of agreement, support, and cooperation. The result is a decision that may or may not be effective.

Decision making is pretty messy. To make the best decisions, you have to "decide how to decide" and weigh a number of factors. You then have to be aware of and overcome some hardwired decision-making biases that confound even the best school executives. Two decision-making factors involve recognition that you can be derailed by either *content decisions* or *decision-making* processes.

Types of Decisions—Content versus Process

Your job, as a school executive, is to make decisions on a daily basis. In fact, some research (Peterson, 2001) suggests that school executives have upward of 50 to 60 interactions each hour. Principals get information, review the facts and data, come up with ideas, evaluate the ideas, and attempt to implement them. This rational decision model works well with short-term operational decisions (decide and move on). However, you need to be aware of some "decision-making disabilities." This type of dysfunction or blind spot will have a tendency to be magnified when making larger, more strategic decisions. This is particularly true when considering how to allocate scarce resources, such as money and time. This phenomenon can also enter into decisions that impact a large number of people with competing interests, similar to the carpool scenario at the beginning of this section.

When most school leaders think of decisions, they tend to focus upon the content; was the decision the right decision or did the decision produce the desired result? Ironically, for those of you who remember high school precalculus, there is generally a "solution space" where more than one right answer can solve the problem. In addition, the more important the decision is, the more likely it is that you will bring together your best minds to try to get at the "right answer." Unfortunately, if you ignore the decision-making process, you may end up with getting a right answer the first time, while demoralizing and frustrating those whom you most want to succeed and empower. This lessens your chances to leverage your team's skills and talents and increases time commitment. In addition, the more unfamiliar the situation, the more likely it is that you are going to tip toward an autocratic mode of decision making when a more participative process will yield a better result. A significant amount of research initiated by Victor Vroom and validated by over 100 other research studies (contingency theory) strongly suggest that there are situations in which participation increases decision effectiveness and in others a more autocratic decision making style is appropriate.

Biases That Hinder Decision Making

Students with specific learning disabilities are often taught to work around or overcome their disabilities So too, principals need to understand, learn, and apply strategies that help leaders overcome biases that hinder decision making. These behaviors are referred to as *anchoring*, *status quo*, and *confirming evidence biases*. (Bazerman & Moore, 2008; Hammond, Keeney, & Raiffa 2002; Lovallo & Kahneman, 2003).

Anchoring Bias

You may know this more readily as the power of the first impression. Our rational minds give disproportionate weight to the first information we receive. All additional information is anchored around that initial information. You see it when you interview teachers. You look at the individual's GPA or where they went to school. You invite them in and ask them some difficult questions. If the candidate had a high GPA or went to a prestigious school, but they don't answer your interview questions effectively, it is quite easy to say "He just had a bad day" or "I guess she just doesn't interview well, but she looks well qualified on paper." Another example is when you consult your leadership team, asking them, "What do you think about issue X?" Their responses might tend to anchor your responses on what you think about the issue.

To work around this bias, consciously view issues or problems from different perspectives before honing in on the first thoughts that come to your mind. You also want to think about the issue on your own before you engage others in asking their opinions. When seeking input, ask a wide variety of people with different backgrounds to get alternative (some might call them "way-out") viewpoints. Finally, avoid inadvertently anchoring those around you in their decisions. When you say "I think that . . . " you can be sure that others will anchor their thoughts and decisions around your thoughts and ideas.

Status Quo Bias

Another root for bias can be found in our need to keep things as they are. If we change our decision, it is an admission that our previous decision was wrong. Most of us hate to admit that we are wrong about anything. If we break from the status quo, we have to act, take responsibility for both our action and our previous decision, and open ourselves to criticism. Political candidates use this bias frequently when they accuse their opponent of flip-flopping on previous decisions. The auto and life insurance industry is based upon the value of maintaining the status quo. How frequently do you shop for life or auto insurance? You have to take time to research the different companies, their coverage levels, and rates. You also have to check their financial backing. After all, if you need auto insurance, you want to ensure that the money is available.

In schools, adults are often reluctant to change and prefer to maintain the status quo out of convenience and familiarity. We do not have to look hard to find examples such as how we use time, assign students to classes, or openness to new pedagogy. Little doubt, then, that you would rather just keep doing what you were doing before you were forced into all of these decisions and had to take responsibility for them. You can take steps to work around this flavor of decision-making disability. Remember that the status quo may be the best decision but that you don't want to choose the current decision simply because it is easy. Look at other options then weigh the advantages and disadvantages of each option, including the status quo. You can also ask, "If the status quo was one of the alternatives and I had to do it over again, would I choose the same option?"

Confirming Evidence Bias

Imagine that you are the principal of a rapidly growing middle school and you have to make some alterations to the master schedule. For a while you've been concerned about ensuring that students get a better "shake" with the elective sign-up process, and you've read of a school in another district that has come up with a new process for elective selection. You talk with one of your colleagues in your system who makes a strong case that what the other district does won't work here. If you take his word as the final arbiter, you've fallen victim to the confirming evidence bias. This bias leads you to seek out only data that supports the decision that you made. It affects the data you gather, how you gather and interpret the data, and ultimately, your decisions. This bias pushes us to give more weight to data that supports your decision and too little weight to any conflicting information. The most egregious instance of this bias is when you make a decision, and then try to find reasons to justify why you made that decision.

To reduce the chances of succumbing to this bias, you have to enlist help. Ask another person to serve as the devil's advocate against your idea. This hurts because the more you advocate for a position, the more difficult it is to have someone question that decision. Better yet, serve as your own devil's advocate. What is the strongest reason to support this decision? Then turn the table and ask what the strongest reason to *not* support this position. Make that list of advantages and disadvantages before you share your ideas with others. Finally, avoid asking leading questions, such as, "Don't you think that . . .?" which might invite the other person to confirm what you are proposing.

Overcoming Decision-Making Disabilities

You know the common blind spots in decision making. This next section gives you hints and tools to reduce your risk of succumbing to these blind spots. You'll also find some tools to help you use group and individual decision-making styles more effective.

Situational Factors

Contingency theory suggests that there are situational factors that affect the appropriate levels of participation. In this section, we discuss capacity, commitment, and alignment.

Capacity refers to the leader's and group's expertise. For example, you've brought your leadership team subcommittee together to try to determine the annual budget. You've done the budget before and have learned some key points that have to be weighted when preparing the budget. However, it is your team's first time to be involved in the budget process (either by new group members or your desire to get greater buy-in and understanding of the budget process). The more expertise you have and the less expertise the group has, the more directive you should likely be. This doesn't mean that you simply decide and let people know what your decision is. It may mean breaking the budget down into much smaller chunks (say field trip budget or professional development budget) and providing some fairly narrow parameters that the team should consider.

However, if you don't have as much knowledge or expertise in an area and the group has greater expertise, you should enlist more participation during the decision-making process. If you are considering a textbook adoption, you assume that the grade or department has more content knowledge than you do of what is needed in new textbook and ancillary materials. You may have some strong ideas on some aspects that need to be a part of the adopted textbook, such as high levels of student engagement, hands-on activities, and ability to differentiate instruction, but you don't want to make that decision in isolation.

When group *commitment* to a decision is important, the more input you need to solicit before you make a decision. Regarding textbook adoption, teachers will be using the materials and textbooks on a daily basis. They need to have significant input in the selection of the textbook ultimately adopted. On the other hand, if it is likely that the group would make the same decision that you would make alone, the more likely it is that *you* can make the decision with little fallout from your team. An example of this is determining which type of copier to lease. Most teachers want a copier without a lot of features: it must be fast, reliable, and have the ability to collate, staple and print on both sides. The brand and type is immaterial to them.

Finally, consider the degree of *alignment*: If your group is closely aligned with the objectives or results at stake, you should invite their participation in the decision-making process. On the other hand, the bigger the gap between organizational goals and individual objectives, the more directive you will have to be. For example, nobody likes lunch, hall, or bus duty. If teachers could get out of it, they would. While you may want to solicit input from them on what factors need to be taken into consideration, you will need to retain the final decision to ensure equity and equality.

The Gap Between Decisions and Action

We've worked with several school leadership teams that struggled with making a decision. The debates were strong, people worked with various alternatives, and finally a decision was made. They then sat back and thought their work was done. After a short while, people started wondering what happened to the result of the decision. It seemed that people knew what needed to be done, but for some reason, nothing actually happened. Pfeffer and Sutton (2000) outline five fundamental problems with moving from decision making to action.

1. Talk Substitutes for Action

One of the main barriers to turning knowledge into action is the tendency to treat *talking* about something as equivalent to actually *doing* something about it. You have likely been in a mind-numbing meeting, where at the meeting's conclusion, someone asks, "So what's the next step?" The response that exemplifies talk substituting for action is, "We need to think deeply about this and come back to meet again."

2. **Making Decisions Substitutes for Action**

Often there seemed to be an unspoken, yet powerful belief that once a decision had been made, no additional work was needed to ensure it was implemented. Schools are particularly adept at this fundamental problem, primarily because we think "school people" are so busy we simply assume that once it is decided, it is done and we can move on to the next crisis.

3. **Preparing Documents Substitutes for Action**

Sutton and Pfeffer found many instances where planning activities, holding meetings to discuss problems and their solutions, and preparing written reports are mistaken for actually accomplishing something. We remember the gut-wrenching hours spent working with school leadership teams of struggling schools to develop school improvement plans. When we came back for a return engagement a month later, we brought our copy of the school improvement plan and started talking with the principal and one of the lead teachers. When we asked them how they were doing with the strategies they outlined in the school improvement plan, they told us that the plan was just a plan—they had more important things to do. Sadly, the children at that school were unable to show achievement gains on the state-mandated tests.

4. **Mission Statements Substitute for Action**

Mission statements are among the most blatant and common means that organizations use to substitute talk for action. They saw many examples of executives acting as if these statements had magical powers to satisfy customers, increase quality, and make employees happier and more productive, almost as a "talisman, hung in public places, to ward off evil spirits" (pp. 37–40).

5. **Planning Substitutes for Action**

People frequently confuse developing a plan as actually implementing the plan. There is little connection between the amount of time and effort an organization devotes to planning compared to how well it performs. If you have a plan collecting dust on the bookshelf, then you have fallen in the gap between planning and action (Pfeffer and Sutton, 2000, pp. 40–42).

Effective Rational Decision-Making Criteria

Think through four questions before embarking on your decision-making process:

1. **Decision Quality:** Will the decision fit within the "solution space' that you have laid out earlier in the process? Will it meet the end results that you are trying to accomplish?

2. **Implementation:** Are group members committed to the decision? Do they have a full understanding of what the decision entails? Will they be able to effectively carry out the decision?

3. **Time Urgency:** How quickly does the decision need to be made? Will making this decision take more time from each individual than it is worth? How important is it to get the input from different groups? Do you have the time available to get this input?

4. **Development:** Will the decision-making process help in developing the talent for future issues within your organization? Will this process enrich their feeling of being a valued and important part of the group or will it be considered simply perfunctory input?

Final Tips

Finally, we'd like to outline some decision-making tips that we have learned over the years.

Transparency matters. Always outline and discuss your decision-making processes. For example, you may announce that the professional development committee owns the professional development budget and activities. This group will decide how your staff development funds will be spent this year. They will also decide how much the school will spend for conferences this year versus having focused staff development within the school. You will be the main character of a horror story if you change the decision-making process midway through the problem because you were uncomfortable with the direction the decision-making process was taking.

Practice new decision-making styles with low-risk decisions first. Don't initiate a new decision-making model on a high-risk decision. Instead, have the group work through the inevitable issues associated with new decision-making models on a lower-risk decision. For example, you don't want your leadership team's first foray into participation to be the overall school budget for the upcoming year.

Teach your teams that the meeting is over only when there are action items. You need to establish the discipline with all of your teams that meetings result in action. Spend the last 5 minutes outlining who will do what by a certain date. Also spend time determining how decisions within the meeting will be communicated to the entire faculty and staff within 24 hours after the close of the meeting.

Be there. Attend those meetings when you are working to develop your team or you have some team members who exhibit dysfunctional behavior. Dysfunctional behavior can include:

♦ Holding team members hostage in the meeting until they get their way

♦ Going off on a sidetrack that derails the meeting

♦ Being passive aggressive (not expressing opinions and being unwilling to support compromise)

Define your parameters. Set your parameters at the beginning of each meeting. This may be related to your strategy (all professional development for the year must tie directly to the school improvement plan or areas of weakness with student achievement) or resource allocation (15% of our instructional supply funds will be spent on items that address our student achievement gaps). You empower a team to make decisions by setting up these parameters at the start.

Hold After-Action Reviews. Perform an after-action review after each major decision or meeting to review what went well and what needs to be improved in both content and process. Instituting this standard after each decision may help avoid what Alan MacCormack calls "superstitious learning." Superstitious learning occurs when decisions are reviewed only if the result or consequence of the decision was negative. (MacCormack, 2004).

10
Making Meetings Work

A new principal followed a fairly standard practice for calling staff meetings. He created an agenda and sent it to everybody before the meeting. He couldn't figure out why they never got past the first few agenda items. Many times the meeting got stuck on the first or second item. Meetings were a mess: nothing got done, nobody liked these meetings, and they were universally hated (especially by the principal). Next, the new principal decided to get teacher input into the meetings and asked people to submit agenda items prior to the meetings. He hoped that including staff input would help the meetings go more smoothly, but they still never got through the agenda; nothing got done and nobody liked these meetings either. So the new principal continued searching for ways to create more effective in meetings. He looked at the way that other principal meetings were run, and he saw a similar situation: long agendas, people droning on and on, getting bogged down in details of agenda items that should have taken 2 minutes, and nothing getting done.

After a seminar on delegation, he had his lead secretary fashion the agenda and give it to him to approve and/or revise. Although he felt that he was "giving something up that was important," he knew it was something that she could do and do well. His lead secretary generated the agenda and added time frames in parentheses to help keep people on track. A typical faculty meeting agenda had agenda items like updates on changes in bus routes, a review of the purchasing guidelines, an update from a conference a teacher attended as part of her professional development, a discussion on the upcoming textbook adoption, and possible grant opportunities—all items to be covered within 60 minutes after school, which was the established weekly faculty meeting time. The posted agenda and timeframes helped a little but were still unsatisfactory; nothing got done and nobody liked them. The most biting comment came from a teacher whom the new principal overheard muttering to another teacher as they came into the meeting, saying, "These meetings are like foam on beer . . . they sound and look good but there is nothing to them. I can't wait to get this meeting over with so we can get some *real* work done." That stinging comment motivated the principal to learn more about what good meetings look like, sound like, and how productive meetings can lead to results.

There are over 25 million meetings in the United States every day. Some of these meetings are ad hoc and impromptu, but the hope is the same: people want meetings that are worthwhile, that start and end on time, and produce results. This chapter focuses on ways that you can make your meetings more effective and results oriented.

Different Meetings for Different Purposes

When we work with school executives on ways to improve the way they run meetings for increased results, we ask them to bring agendas from their past year's faculty meetings. When we ask them to analyze the agendas, a couple of interesting trends emerge.

Agenda items are frequently set by one or two ways: either by historical precedent or by crisis. Every August, there are the myriad of back-to-school agenda items that have been deemed critical to the start of school. In October, school principals start the budgeting process to go to the superintendent in February. Every March there is a flurry of activity to complete the observations and evaluations that are due to human resources. Many school executives end up with an agenda that looks like stew. The individual ingredients may taste good by themselves or in combination with a couple of other ingredients, but when you put conflicting ingredients together, you get a stew that looks bad and tastes bad. This is "meeting mush," a bad mix of different agenda items like monthly goals, administrative details, and big picture ideas. Alone, they are important items worthy of a place on the agenda. Together, they taste terrible when they are mixed without a sense of how they tie together.

Less effective meetings try to blend disparate elements by attempting to get small administrative elements out of the way early. They get sidetracked and stuck on those administrative details so that the meeting never gets around to the important stuff. This frustrates everyone. The most effective executives separate the operational elements from those that are more strategic by clearly differentiating their meeting agendas among strategic, operational issues, and updates. By delineating these items on the agenda, the leader creates a steady drumbeat that everybody knows about upfront. Let's take a look at the different types of meetings, their purposes, and effective leadership behaviors in each type of situation.

Strategy versus Operations

Pat Lencioni (2004) gives this type of analogy to bolster the case for separating strategy from operations. Imagine that you have two TV's going on, both of which have the *picture in picture* feature (where you can view two shows on the same screen at the same time). Could you follow the plot of trying to watch "Driving Miss Daisy" and the sitcom "Full House" at the same time that the other TV has the President of the United States delivering the State of the Union and a basketball game going on with the picture in picture on the other TV? It doesn't make much sense. That's similar to trying to have a meeting analyzing student achievement scores, discussing field trip requirements for transportation, and reviewing a new school board policy that impacts the individual school. Be sure to separate the content of different meetings to separate strategy versus operations. Let's take a look at the different types of operational meetings that you can use to make meetings work.

Operations and Effective Leadership: The 5-Minute Stand-Up Meeting

The first type of meeting is a daily stand-up meeting. We first learned of this meeting from the 24-hour news channel, CNN. They held a 15-minute meeting every day where the key people who produce the programs talk about what they are focusing on during the upcoming day (Peters, 1996). That they do this every day for 15 minutes in a chaotic, fast-breaking news environment to keep everybody up to speed fascinated us. We don't advocate that you allot 15 minutes if you don't need that much time. You may find that 5-minute meeting consisting of you, your assistant principal(s), and your lead secretary is sufficient. This daily meeting at the beginning of each day serves as a check in to see what is going on and to ensure that nothing falls between the cracks. We're partial to doing this in the morning before the buses arrive. Routine topics might include which teachers are out and have a substitute (and which classes still need a sub), whether there are any field trips, assemblies, guest speakers, visitors in the building, or extraordinary activities going on that day. If there are issues that have not been caught, you have the chance to assign them and keep the instructional day as uninterrupted as possible. You may think it works better for you to do this meeting during the day or at the end of the day. Whatever you choose, keep these point in mind:

1. Hold the meeting even if everybody cannot be there. Even if there are only two of you at that meeting, that brief check-in can yield substantial dividends to reduce the number of emergencies that come up during the day.

2. Keep the meeting length to 300 seconds. Don't allow the meeting to dawdle and lengthen to 10 or 15 minutes. The key concern is what needs to happen in the next 8 hours. It is not for lengthy discourse. You can use a kitchen timer set for 5 minutes to help everyone be succinct and concise.

3. Make this a stand-up meeting. Don't allow anybody to sit down. There is something about sitting down that makes the idea of a longer meeting more palatable. Resist this impulse. Keep people standing and keep them to the allotted 5 minutes to stay on top of those nitty gritty operational details without eating up a lot of time.

Some schools have implemented a similar type of meeting within grade levels or departments, just to do a check in with each other. This is obviously more difficult if you have a department, team, or grade level that is spread out on a large campus or multistory building.

The biggest advantage to this daily stand-up is saving time by taking time. This meeting saves time by reducing e-mail traffic among all of you, avoids questions like "Is Pat (the roving instructional coach) in today?," "Who is attending the IEP meeting this afternoon?," and "Which of us is sitting in on the 8th grade team meeting 3rd period?" This meeting helps avoid confusion, duplication of effort, and stepping on other's toes while it creates a forum to ensure that nothing falls between the cracks.

Your role as a a leader in this meeting is simply to facilitate a round-robin format where you ask each person what is going on that day. You should go last for a couple of reasons:

♦ If time runs out, you can more easily send an e-mail to everybody or jot it down and give it to your team if they are all over the building.

♦ You want to establish and encourage initiative and build capacity within your leadership team. Giving them the chance to establish themselves and build their skills in ad hoc leadership discussions can help build their capacity. If somebody has a question that does not involve the entire group, encourage them to discuss it separately.

Operations and Effective Leadership: Weekly Ops Review

Lencioni (2004) discusses a tool called the Weekly Ops Review. This meeting serves as a forum to ensure that you get a status update on the critical initiatives in the school improvement plan. The meeting agenda is directly based upon progress on those initiatives. Lencioni suggests that this meeting can occur weekly or every other week and lasts no more than an hour. We've seen this type of meeting work well both with the principal's leadership team (assistant principal, guidance counselor, and possibly the lead secretary) or the school's leadership team (grade or department level leaders). Some schools have adapted this for their individual department or grade level team meetings. The template below, Figure 10.1, can be adapted to fit your needs. First, we will review each element in the meeting planner worksheet work.

A. **The Lightning Round (5 minutes).** You ask each of the people in the meeting to share in 1 minute what priorities they have been working on during that week or 2-week period. People are generally incredulous that this can be done in a minute per person but when we ask them during our seminars to get in groups of three and share what priorities they are working on, they are amazed that they generally get done well before the 3-minute mark. This lightning round is important because it helps set the tone of the meeting, gives everybody a chance for their "air time" as well as a sense of what others are working on, and it makes it easy to identify redundancies, gaps, and any other issues.

B. **Focus on the KEIs (3 minutes)**. KEIs (pronounced "keys") is an acronym for Key Education Indicators. You can substitute this acronym for whatever acronym your school improvement plan is. The important point is that you have identified the four or five key indicators from your school improvement plan. You spent the time determining what you think will help make your school better and assigned both performance measures and people responsible for those initiatives. Here is where you ask for status reports from people responsible for monitoring or implementing the key indicators within your school improvement plan. Generally these are filled in and do not change from meeting to meeting unless you have changed the performance metric overall or the metric and initiative is successfully completed. The second part of this meeting is to simply ask—for each of the five key indicators—whether you are behind, on track, doing better than the metric (ahead), or if it is unknown. This second part of the meeting gives the structure and sets the agenda for the rest of the meeting. As the leader you want to maintain focus on the key indicators and look for people to report on the progress (or lack of progress) with these indicators. Total time thus far—8 minutes.

C. **The Weekly Agenda (30 to 40 minutes).** The information gained from the lightning round and the review of the KEIs sets the agenda for the rest of the meeting. If there are areas where progress is not as expected, then that becomes an agenda item. If there are areas of accelerated progress, there is no need to spend time on it unless you want to see if there are lessons that can be leveraged to other areas. Once you determine what the topics are, you then prioritize them (the Order column in section C), and get closure on the most important item (the #1 priority) and don't move on until the #1 issue is resolved or the next steps assigned. Time: 30 minutes. Total time: 38–48 minutes

D. **Possible Strategic Issues (approx. 1 minute at most).** Frequently, items come up that are not operational or don't hit the KEIs. Someone thinks of an important topic and wants to bring it up during the weekly ops review. *Don't* let them. This is what gets many leaders in trouble. Instead, jot it down in section D—Possible Strategic Issues. This is a "parking lot" of possible agenda items to discuss. Many times, these items can be resolved "off line" or dealt with during the next step (E). Sometimes these issues require a separate ad hoc meeting of two or three individuals, which is fine. The key is to have that meeting for that particular issue alone—don't engage in meeting mush.

E. **Decisions and Actions (5 minutes).** After each agenda item has been discussed, identify action steps, who is responsible, and the timeline for each. This also serves as the focus for the next meeting's lightning round to ensure that what was assigned gets done. Total time: 43–53 minutes.

F. **Communication Plan (5 minutes).** Here is where you ensure that everybody knows what and how they are going to communicate the results of the meeting to the groups that they represent. *Don't shortchange this portion of the meeting.* People are always curious about what is going on "behind closed doors." This is especially true if you are implementing and holding people accountable for what is in the school improvement plan. Total time: 48–58 minutes.

Figure 10.1   Weekly Ops Review

A) 60 Second Priority Roundtable	B) KEI Review					
	Goal	Metric	Behind	On Track	Ahead	Unknown
	1.					
	2.					
	3.					
	4.					
	5.					

C) Tactical Agenda Items

Order	Topic

	D) Potential Strategic Topics

E) Decisions/Actions

Who	What	When

F) Communication Plan

Adapted from Lencioui, P. (224). *Death By Meeting.* San Francisco: Jossey-Bass.

Operations and Effective Leadership: Monthly Focus

This meeting can occur monthly, every other month, or quarterly. It is a meeting that takes care of one of the issues that have been raised in the weekly ops review or as part of your strategy sessions. Many school principals use this format if they have a schoolwide planning meeting of parents, teachers, and community members. These meetings, we have found, can be the most interesting and most important.

We recommend that you focus on only one major topic during this meeting. It is seductive and alluring to succumb to pressure from your teachers who say, "We are going to meet for two hours. Let's get through at least three topics at this time." Resist this temptation. Instead, force the distillation of one key issue for you and the team. This format will help you experience success by wrestling with critical issues, analyzing data, debating solutions, and reaching consensus.

Sull (2007) outlines the four stages and effective leadership behaviors and questions for each stage (see Figure 10.2).

FIGURE 10.2 Four Steps of Effective Leadership Behavior

Stage	Leadership Behaviors
Making Sense	Inquiry, curiosity, empathy to see other view, challenge assumptions, ensure full discussion by all members in the group
	Key Question: "What fresh data would convince us that our assessment is inaccurate?"
Making Choices	Respectful argumentation (disagree with the position, not the person)
	Schoolwide perspective vs. parochial self-interests
	Determine prioritization rules for decision making among various possibilities.
	Determine performance measures publicly
	Key Question: "What will we stop doing?" (emphasis added)
Making It Happen	Supportive monitoring (possibly using the template for the weekly ops review)
	Publicly monitor performance (group and peer pressure)
	Link promises to priorities
	Key Question: "What did you promise to do? What have you done? What is hindering you?"
Making Revisions	Dispassionate rational analysis
	Intellectual humility
	Respect for other viewpoints
	Sensitivity to anomalies
	Key Questions: "What did we expect to happen vs. what actually happened? Why the difference? What should we change?"

We've learned a couple of other tips that will help you in these meetings:

Have the data and information for the meeting at least a week ahead of time. You want this meeting to be a decision-making meeting, not a discussion meeting. You also want to set the expectation that the meeting time will not be used to rehash what could have been read ahead of time.

Lencioni suggests that one way to determine topics for this monthly focus meeting is to have everybody write down one issue that they think would be good for the next focus meeting. Call them out one by one and put them on a white board. If more than one person has the same or similar idea, don't put it down repeatedly. Then before you have the team vote for what should be the focus, you want everybody to get 60 seconds to pitch their idea for the monthly focus. Then you call for the question. Everybody gets two votes and they can use them for one choice (2 votes) or split them between two different proposals. Here's the twist. The individuals cannot vote for their own idea. Once the decision is made on what the topic is, then send everybody back and have them turn in data or research or information that can be shared with the entire group a week before the meeting takes place.

Making Meetings Work—Lessons Learned

We'll close this chapter with some various lessons we've learned from our work and from various sources. Use these lessons to help ensure that your meetings stay on track and focus on your priorities.

- **Keep your focus**. Focus on what you want to accomplish and use meetings to maintain that same focus for others in your school.

- **Stay involved.** You can and should delegate as much as you can to get more discretionary time to focus on your priorities. Stay involved, however, in your key initiatives and don't delegate the management of these meetings to another person on your staff. Your presence or non-presence speaks volumes about your priorities.

- **Have simple follow-up mechanisms.** The meeting template earlier in the chapter is a two-page running record of all of your key decisions and who is keeping up with each of them.

- **Rotate and donate.** Be purposeful in leading the meetings. At the same time you are driving results, you want to increase the capabilities of your team. Periodically assign others the role of running the meeting and you simply sit in. Rotate the role after you have worked out the kinks in how you want meetings managed. Prep the individual ahead of time so that he or she is not surprised by your request to have that person lead the meeting.

- **Avoid verbal memos.** We're surprised by the number of principals who would use faculty meetings to send verbal memos—5 minutes of telling people what needed to happen or an information dump. You've hired very highly qualified and literate people. Don't waste meeting time sharing one-way information on policies or procedures, carpool changes or changes in the lunch schedule. Simply write it down, send it out, and save your meeting time for sharing ideas, getting feedback, and moving forward on your agenda.

♦ **Have a sense of the dramatic.** There will be times when you have a meeting and before you get to the end of the agenda, someone has something significant to celebrate. When that big moment comes and the faculty are amped up over it, adjourn the meeting and have the faculty walk out on a high. You'll have other opportunities to get your message across.

♦ **Watch your tense.** One technique you may use in your observations is listening to the kinds of questions that teachers ask, according to Bloom's or Marzano's levels of thinking. The same kind of analysis can be applied to you. Tape record yourself or have a trusted colleague (secretary, assistant principal, or teacher) run a tally list on how much of your conversation or meetings are focused on what happened today versus what happened in the past (which we will argue is pretty counterproductive since you can't relive the past) and how much of the conversation is forward-looking— what we are going to do tomorrow. Want to get real obsessive about it? Ask that same person to jot down the verbs that are used—are they backward focused or forward focused?

♦ **"Let's review."** Make sure you have the last 5 minutes of the meeting to review and recap to ensure that everyone is on the same page, next steps and actions are written down, and due dates are included. Post the minutes via e-mail and in the faculty lounge.

♦ **Cultivate muzzle spasm.** This is pretty obvious, but keep your mouth shut as much as you can. There is an old saying, "When the boss says, 'I think,' the thinking stops." You want to get as much discussion from your team as possible. Put a muzzle on your snout.

11

Keeping Your School in a Positive Light

Today's school leaders have to compete for resources just like other community organizations. Even in the most supportive communities, increasing numbers of taxpayers are asking how their tax dollars are spent. Justification for dollars equates to finding ways to demonstrate how your school is thriving, improving, or effectively using the resources that you have been allocated. In addition, you see the beginning of a tidal wave of teachers being able to retire and the talent pool of young teachers becoming increasingly mobile and technologically sophisticated. These teachers go online for social networking and for help in solving problems, and they have reviewed your school website when preparing for an interview or choosing among different schools to interview.

Given the increasing pressure to showcase their school, principals are told to "market your school," yet the image in many school leaders' minds equate marketing with selling. Selling's image is frequently of a car salesman or TV huckster telling you why you can't live without the product. Marketing is different than selling. Marketing is the art and science of keeping your school in front of people's minds.

Your can spotlight the positives of your school through differentiation, translating features into benefits, tailored communication, and smart marketing with technology.

Differentiation

In today's chaotic school environment, it's more important than ever that you cast your school's strengths in the most positive light. Teachers, parents, and community members have more choices than ever in where to teach, where to send their child, and where to give additional financial support. One of your roles is making your school stand out from other public and private schools so that people want to affiliate with your school.

Schools are obsessed with taking best practices from other schools. Teachers glean ideas from other teachers. School executives take back good ideas from conversations with colleagues at meetings, conferences, and conventions. We benchmark ourselves against other schools and constantly look for best practices that we can share. These are terrific strategies that we should use in improving our instructional programs, our operations, and the way we lead and manage our teams. Unfortunately, when we apply these concepts to marketing the school, we end up looking like everybody else, sounding like everybody else, and acting like everybody else. Potential parents and members of the community may not recognize the difference between your school and all the other schools that are out there competing for the same resources. You have to distinguish your school.

Imagine your responses to a parent who wants to learn more about your school. Whether you are an elementary, middle, or high school principal, this parent will ask the same six general questions. Jot down your responses to this potential parent who comes into your office wanting to know about your school and asks,

- ♦ "Tell me about your teachers."

- ♦ "Tell me about the curriculum at your school."

- ♦ "How are the students at your school? What are they like?"

- ♦ "What sort of instructional focus do you have?"

- ♦ "How committed are the parents at your school?"

- ♦ "Describe how the community is involved in your school."

Over 98% of you would answer these six questions very similarly. The most common responses might be:

- ♦ "Our teachers are caring, committed, very competent, focused, and very highly qualified."

- ♦ "Our curriculum is rigorous. We focus our instruction on a hands-on, very practical approach that helps children learn in a diverse and global economy."

- ♦ "Our students are very, very strong."

- ♦ "Our parents are vital to our success. They stay involved, and our community is a very active participant and partner."

These comments noted above are accurate and fair, but they are just like stacks of vanilla ice cream cartons in the frozen food section of the grocery store. They all look alike. So how do you transform your school from just like everybody else to being a school that is distinctive for the right reasons and for the right things? Think, "Distinct or Extinct" (Peters, 1999a).

Walk around your school or drive around your school district. Visit teachers in their classrooms. Listen to parents and children. Use this time to identify some ways that others think your school is different. Keep a list of all the ways that your school is different. Look for themes as you jot these down. You can also ask these questions of your PTA council, your teachers, and your business partners. These questions should prompt your thinking:

- What is your school famous for?
- What are you most proud of?
- What makes your school unique and distinct?

Benefits—The Power of YOU

Many school executives make a common mistake when beginning their marketing effort. They focus internally upon what their school *does*. This mistake is understandable because you have to be a champion and cheerleader for your school. However, your current and potential stakeholders may not care about the same things that you care about. Your efforts will fall short if you focus solely upon what your school does (features) and fail to translate them into benefits. Your recruiting efforts may dwindle, parents and students may become increasingly apathetic, and community members may lose their enthusiasm for your school.

Find the Benefits in the Features

Some people find it useful to think of the features as the "what" and the benefits as the "why." Another way of thinking of this is that features are *internally focused* (focused on internal processes), while benefits are *externally focused* (focused on what is important to the outside world).

Let's look at two examples of how effective marketing moves from features to benefits. Automated teller machines (ATMs) were designed partly to increase the convenience of having a bank 24 hours a day, 7 days a week, 365 days a year. They filled a need for people to safely withdraw or deposit money after normal banking hours. You might market ATMs by focusing on the "power of you" by saying: "You get convenient and safe banking, wherever you are and whenever you travel."

You can analyze diet cola as a second example. Diet cola is a combination of artificial sweeteners and cola tastes. It comes in a can or bottle similar to that of traditional cola. Diet cola gives you the same taste as regular cola without all the sugar. If you were the marketing manager for diet cola, you might say:

"You get the same taste without all the calories."

When you go to your doctor, you likely see some impressive plaques in the waiting room. One notes that she graduated from a university medical school. Another plaque notes that your doctor is board certified. Still a third plaque notes a letter of commendation from a local university thanking her for helping the athletes. What is the effect of all these impressive looking documents?

"You get a highly qualified and competent physician."

Now let's look at some school examples. The closest parallel to the doctor are your teachers. Almost all of them are highly qualified to teach. What do you want the message to be to your parents and community?

Figure 11.1 Sample Benefits

Product or Service	Benefits
ATM	You get instant access to a bank almost anywhere you are.
Diet drinks	You get all the taste of a regular soda without the calories.
Board certified physician	You get a highly competent doctor.
Highly qualified teacher	Your child gets a very capable, caring and talented teacher who will help her achieve her fullest potential.
Mobile laptop cart	Your child gets the latest technology to prepare for the 21st century.

"You get a very capable, caring, and talented teacher."

Let's say you have recently invested in a wireless laptop mobile cart. One way to market this investment might be:

"Your child has access to the latest technology to prepare for the 21st century."

The chart (see Figure 11.1) summarizes these examples that translate features into benefits. Note how the "power of you" is amplified in each example.

So how does a discussion of features and benefits translate into how you market your schools? Here are the key differences between features and benefits. Features are processes or parts of your school that must be demonstrated to your stakeholders. Features cannot be simply something that you hope to do in the future. Your benefits tie into emotional responses as well as cultural values being addressed.

Let's take reducing class size as an example of how to translate features into benefits. Many schools try to reduce class size. Unfortunately, they don't clearly explain the benefit of reducing class size to the community and taxpayers. What's the benefit to the stakeholders of reducing class size? If you focus only on how reducing class size benefits the teacher, you are focusing upon the wrong stakeholder group. Reducing class size appeals to parents because it provides more personalized attention for their child, and each child can increase their achievement compared with how they achieve in a larger class.

Earlier, you listed features of your school that made your school different and unique. Return to those features and write them down on the left hand side of the chart in Figure 11.2. On the right hand side, now write down how the features help your client. Think in your head, "Here's how (the strength or feature) helps *you* (or *your child*).

For instance, if one of your features is "We have a very rigorous curriculum" and you want to convey that to parents of school-aged children, then you might list your benefit as "My children will be well-prepared for a very complex work environment when they graduate." If your second feature is, "Our teachers are very caring and nurturing," the benefit could be "We help your child feel welcome and safe."

FIGURE 11.2 Moving from Strengths to Benefits

Strengths or features about your school	How the strength/feature helps you (or your child)

Caution! Beware the "So What" Factor

As you end up contrasting your features and benefits between your schools and others, be certain that those benefits matter to your stakeholders. You may have a distinctive benefit that may not create a great deal of positive good will for your school. How important are your benefits? As you develop your benefits for your different target groups, remember that a benefit is only a benefit *in your stakeholders' eyes*. Jeff Thull (2005) suggests that one major barrier to your marketing effort occurs when your list of benefits is irrelevant and of marginal use to your clients. Your benefits must be relevant and important to your different clients and stakeholders. Benefits that are important to different groups are called "Key Drivers."

Key Drivers are benefits that are important to target groups and provide a clear distinction between you and other schools. For example, everybody will say, "We have quality teachers." To make this a Key Driver, don't stop by just saying you have quality teachers. List their qualifications, the number of highly qualified teachers you have, the number and percentage of teachers with an advanced degree or the number and percent who have taken graduate level training (even if it didn't lead to a graduate degree). Other principals have talked about how many nationally board certified teachers they have on staff, or how many of their teachers have presented at state or regional conferences.

To gain a different perspective, let's look at the Yellow Pages advertisements for business services. Begin your search by looking at the advertisements for plumbers. Plumbers, by and large, do not publicize where they went to school or what type of degrees they have obtained. Yet, many plumbers have built thriving businesses competing for the same customers. Almost all plumbers work with stopped up drains, slow water, water leaks, blocked sewers, no hot water, or toilet trouble. But if you look at the advertisements in the phone book for different plumbers, each advertisement tells you very specifically why you should choose that particular plumber to solve your plumbing problem. Their advertisement focuses directly on the problem you have (features) and provides a valuable solution (benefits).

So how does this translate to your school? You need to transform features of your school to benefits that are important to different stakeholders. Whenever you can quantify the benefit, you increase the benefit's effectiveness. See Figure 11.3 for examples of translating features into benefits.

To take advantage of the plumbers' wisdom, create your own yellow pages ad for your school in the box below (see Figure 11.4). Keep four points in mind:

1. Your advertisement is not an art project. Pictures should demonstrate an example of the benefit that you offer.

2. Less is more. Fewer words, focused on benefits, often in a bulleted-type list, are more effective than a long drawn out paragraph.

3. When you review your benefits, be sure to include the key points that are highly distinct about your school, and are very important to your school populations or your target groups.

4. Think bullet points-you don't want to have more than seven words for a benefit. Boil it down until you have 5–7 bullet points, each with seven words.

FIGURE 11.3 Sample Features to Benefits

Feature	Benefit
Our school met most of its No Child Left Behind goals with Annual Yearly Progress.	Our school met 29 out of 30 goals (97%) under No Child Left Behind.
We have high quality teachers.	100% of our teachers are highly qualified. 65% of our faculty has either advanced course work or credentials. Our school has seven nationally board certified teachers.
We have high academic standards.	This past year, our seniors received over $100,000 in scholarships. Graduates were accepted to over 50 different colleges, universities, and military academies..

FIGURE 11.4 Advertisement Worksheet

Tailor Your Message

What you'll note in this section is that there seems to be a multitude of ways that you can market the school—so it seems easy to get overwhelmed. Relax. Remember that there are three to five elements that make your school unique, different, and special. You've honed these features into benefits. The rest of this chapter will provide strategies for sharing those benefits with your stakeholders.

Tailor to Target Groups

When most school executives begin to market their school, they jump immediately to the message they want to send out to the community. These school executives try to illustrate what their school stands for and its strength. This immediate focus on the singular message can result in a message that may not resonate with all of your stakeholders. The first step to tailoring your message is to determine your target groups, and then develop the message around their values.

When you analyze target groups, think of all of the different groups that are affected in your school. You'll see a tool to help you tailor your core message in the three-column worksheet (see Figure 11.5). List the four or five major groups to whom you want to market. You may want to consider these target groups to start your thinking:

+ Elementary and middle school-walkers and car poolers

+ High school students who drive, band boosters, athletic boosters

+ All grade spans of bus riders and children with special needs, new residents, long-time residents, community organizations, business community, and faith-based organizations.

In the middle column, write down what you have heard that each group values. You'll have to make a professional judgment on some of these perceived areas of importance. In many cases, parents have not explicitly told you what it is that they want for their children. For example, you may have a group of parents who see school as threatening or unfair, so it's important to them that their child is treated fairly. Parents of children with special needs want their children to be successful, loved, and nurtured.

In the right hand-side of the column, beside each group, review the benefits you outlined earlier and find ways to customize that benefit to meet that need for your target group. You'll find that several target groups have similar, if not identical needs. This is a way you can create a tailored and customized benefit for each of your stakeholder groups.

Community members represent the *Hidden Market*—citizens who vote but do not have children in your schools. In many cases, almost three-quarters of the registered voters do not have school-age children. In many cases, the hidden market doesn't know what is happening within your school. They want to make sure that their tax dollars are being used effectively and efficiently. They will not vote in favor of a bond issue or a tax increase which they know very little about. School executives have to find ways to tailor

FIGURE 11.5   Tailored Messages for Target Groups

Stakeholder group	What they want or need	How your benefit can be tailored to what they want
The Hidden Market		

their message that includes this hidden market and keeps them involved. This group of stakeholders will become increasingly important as more people retire and seek to be active, informed, and involved. If you want the Hidden Market's support, you have to help them know how to connect with and support your school.

Moments of Truth

Parents who come to visit your school have approximately five or six contacts with frontline school employees. In most schools, these people are the secretary, the teacher, the principal, the assistant principal, the parking lot supervisor or the school resource officer, the cafeteria workers, and the custodians. Former Scandinavian Airlines chief, Jan Carlzon, calls these informal, nonscripted contacts "moments of truth." To your parent or to the student, each of these five or six people is the entire school—notwithstanding that it is "non-rational" to think that a person forms an opinion of an entire school with approximately 100 employees based upon only the five or six people with whom a person comes in contact. To make the most of these moments of truth, ask these questions:

♦ When you walk into a school, what do you notice?

♦ Are the floors and walls clean?

♦ Is the secretary behind a tall wall, like a moat to the medieval castle? or is it open and inviting to anybody who comes in?

♦ Are the hallways clean?

- ◆ Do people call parents back within 24 hours or e-mail them within 24 hours, even if there is nothing to report?

- ◆ Do all school employees greet parents and greet the students with smiles on their faces, or mostly snarls or grimaces?

All of these are moments of truth for the school. They are critically important to you in terms of marketing your school. If you don't have these critical pieces in place first, all the amount of marketing in the world will not improve the school's image in the community.

Messages: One-Way or Two-Way

Philip Kotler (2006) differentiates *one-way marketing* from *interactive marketing*. Kotler describes one-way marketing as brochures, newsletters, and e-mails. Interactive types of marketing include websites, PTO or PTA meetings, presentations, open houses, meet-the-teacher nights, and various short, ad hoc conversations that you have with different groups. You need a plan that addresses both one-way messages as well as interactive messages, or two-way messages, to get the most from marketing efforts.

One-way messages: These have a distinct advantage because they can be prepared ahead of time. Examples are monthly newsletters, presentations to PTA/PTSO meetings, and brochures that you have in your office to publicize events—all terrific sources of marketing.

Tracy Lewis, a North Carolina principal, uses her fax cover sheet as a very effective one-way tool to market school events. We've adapted the cover sheet, changed the name of the school and the mascot, and included some benefits to re-emphasize the benefits of interests to potential stakeholders (see Figure 11.6). The vast majority of faxes will go to community members, business partners, the media, PTA officers, and the central office. (Note: all names, mascots, phone numbers, and website addresses are fictitious.)

Two-way interactions: Two-way interactions are those seemingly random and ad hoc conversations you may have with somebody while supervising morning or afternoon duty, in the store, or in the parking lot. These are all possible opportunities for you to share your message. Tom Peters (1999 b) notes that the golden rule in today's chaotic world is "He Who Has The Best Story, Wins." You should be able to tell your story in a parking lot speech.

A parking lot speech is a way of conveying your school's message during a brief encounter. Your parking lot speech is basically a summary of what is going on within your school, what's important about your school, and how it helps the community, all done within one minute. Imagine you are in a parking lot getting out of your car and parked right next to you is an elected official in your community. You both get out going into the same building and the elected official goes to you and says, "So, tell me about your school." To create your parking lot speech, look at your benefits and stakeholders, and then craft a short speech that you can essentially commit to memory and give whenever someone asks you, "What's going on with your school?" You can extend this to a one or three-minute speech with more detail, simply by offering specific examples for each of your benefits.

FIGURE 11.6   Sample Fax Cover Sheet

FAX

Pinnacle High School
101 Scenic View Lane
Mountain Top, NC 01010
(v) 000-347-3268 "Wld Cats"
(f) 000-327-2687 "Wld Cats"
One of three Schools of Distinction in the
Mountain Ridge County School System

To: _____

Fax # _____

From: Pat Metot, Principal

Date: _____/_____/_____

Number of pages (incl cover sheet) _____

Remarks:

◊ Urgent

◊ For Your Review

◊ Reply ASAP

◊ Per Your Request

Message/Comments

_____

_____

_____

_____

_____

DID YOU KNOW?

◊ **Pinnacle High** School was recognized as a High School of Distinction by the State Education Department in 2003-04 (one of 10 awarded statewide)

◊ **Pinnacle** High School met 29 of 30 goals set under the federal No Child Left Behind laws.

◊ **Pinnacle** High School has 7 Nationally Board Certified Teachers

◊ **Pinnacle** High School has 100% of their teachers identified as "highly qualified" under state and federal requirements

◊ **Pinnacle** High School has 60% of faculty with either advanced coursework or credentials.

◊ **Pinnacle** High School earned the High School Athletic Association's Sportsmanship Cup

◊ **Pinnacle** High School is fully accredited by the Consolidated Association of Colleges and Schools

◊ Pinnacle High School's seniors last year received over $800,000 in scholarships from public and private colleges and universities.

Visit our website:
http://www.mountainridge.k12.us.pinnacle

Annual Marketing Plan

Enlisting an individual or small team can help you create an effective annual marketing plan. Identify several staff members who possess good communication skills and like promoting the school in the community. The following menu will be helpful in getting them started:

- ◆ Newspaper articles placed in local publications

- ◆ Speaking engagements for civic organizations. Your local civic organizations and service fraternities and sororities are all looking for speakers at their weekly or monthly meetings

- ◆ Open House

- ◆ Realtor Open House

- ◆ Back to School Night

- ◆ Fall Festival/Carnival

- ◆ PTO Meetings

- ◆ School Newsletter

- ◆ Website

On the next two pages, you'll see both a sample annual marketing plan template, Figure 11.7, and a blank template, Figure 11.8. In the top portion of the page, describe some of the ways you market the school. In the bottom section, put a / (slash) in the months that you want to make sure you do something with the marketing of your school. Meet monthly on the status of different activities. Put another slash (\) through the item when it is completed, thereby creating an "X". The annual marketing plan allows you to monitor what has been done on one sheet of paper. The sample marketing plan is a status update for the month of December. You'll note that all planned activities from July until December have an "X" and that two items (website and school newsletter) have not yet been completed.

Don't Let Technology Make You Look Stupid

Almost every school has a website. Schools without an up-to-date website may even be considered inferior. Unfortunately, in many schools, the website was created with less regard for the content than what is technically possible. The best websites may reflect the talents of the webmaster, but the overall plan for the website should remain with the school executive. There is an abundance of information on what makes a good website that we have summarized below (for example, see Nielson, 2005). Armed with this information, you can ensure that the school's website becomes a terrific marketing tool to help stakeholders better understand the school's values and strengths.

FIGURE 11.7 Annual Marketing Plan Template (Sample)

Number	Description
1	Open House
2	Realtor Open House
3	Back To School Night
4	Fall Festival/Spring Carnival
5	Website
6	School Newsletter
7	PTO meeting
8	Civic group/service organization speaker
9	
10	
11	
12	
13	
14	

	Jul	Aug	Sept	Oct	Nov	Dec	Jan	Feb	Mar	Apr	May	Jun
1		X					/					
2				X				/				
3			X									
4				X						/		
5	X	X	X	X	X	/	/	/	/	/	/	/
6			X	X	X		/	/	/	/	/	/
7			X			X			/		/	
8	X	X	/	/	/	/	/	/	/	/	/	/
9												
10												
11												
12												
13												
14												

Figure 11.8   Annual Marketing Plan Template

Number	Description
1	
2	
3	
4	
5	
6	
7	
8	
9	
10	
11	
12	
13	
14	

	Jul	Aug	Sept	Oct	Nov	Dec	Jan	Feb	Mar	Apr	May	Jun
1												
2												
3												
4												
5												
6												
7												
8												
9												
10												
11												
12												
13												
14												

Top Mistakes That Websites Make (see Nielson, 2005)

1. Neglecting the user's point of view: Weak websites focus on "Me, me, me." Their creators forget to take time to find out what their clients want. Your first decision needs to be to determine what you want the website to do. Do you want it to simply be an electronic version of your parent handbook? Do you want it to be interactive? Neither answer is wrong, but you should take into consideration what users want as well as how much time and resources can be devoted to maintaining the website (see item 3 below).

2. It's a website, not an electronic melting pot. Weak websites seem to reflect the notion that everything happening at school is web-worthy and should be put up on the website. You should place some items on the website where people can either download or get questions answered without calling the school. Some examples of these might include your school calendar, special events at the school, starting and ending times, and frequently asked questions. *Do not place sensitive or security information on your website.* One chilling example was a school website that put their school's floor plan on the website. Safety and security experts strongly discourage placing that sensitive information on the web.

3. It's not "One and Done." Websites are interactive by nature and should have information updated frequently. If you have time-sensitive information that has not been updated in 6 months, then your stakeholders will note a lack of attention to detail and project that to other aspects of your school as well.

4. Forget about the cool index: In a 2004 survey, Customer Respect Group, Inc. (April 2004) reported that 54% of those who abandoned a website during a 3-month study period cited "lack of simplicity" as the motive; 70% said that they would go to another site if it was easier to use. The message is to keep it simple and easy to use. Don't use a technology "just because it's cool."

When you evaluate your website, you should take a look at two major areas: 1) navigation/design/layout and 2) content.

1. Navigation, design, and layout—the "how it looks" aspect of your website

♦ **What matters most?** The most important information about your school or about that webpage should be "above the fold." In a newspaper, the day's headline and top story is above the fold. This axiom also applies to websites. Don't make people scroll for that information.

♦ **Make it clear!** Strive for a very clear and consistent design format. All web links should be the same (vertical or horizontal) on every webpage. Avoid having your navigation bars along the vertical axis on some web pages, and across the horizontal axis on others.

♦ **Make it pop!** Links should be large and clearly identified as links. Links and website background should have high color contrast for easy visibility.

- ◆ **Make it work!** Be sure that the links work. Every month or so, go on your website and just randomly click through to make sure that links do link to the page you want them to.

- ◆ **Make it quick!** Pages should load in 6 seconds or less. Stakeholders may click the back button and ignore the website if your pages take longer to load. The most common culprit with long loading pages is graphics. Graphics must be *compressed* so that links will not take long to load. This is especially important in the more rural areas without broadband access.

- ◆ **Make It "Three Clicks and You're In"!** Easy access is another principle of good website design. No doubt you have been frustrated searching for information or a document on a website. A good rule of thumb: It should take no more than three clicks to navigate the site and find the most important information and major events. Solicit feedback from people who view and use the site.

2. Content

- ◆ **Proofread.** Every word on your website should be grammatically correct and there should be no typos.

- ◆ **Know what is important to users.** Make sure the content on your website is important and valuable to client groups. If you want to test whether the content is important, ask potential users of your website what they think is important information.

- ◆ **Don't play "Where's Waldo?"** Critical information should be posted on the opening home page of your website, including mailing address, the street address, phone number, the starting and ending times of classes, and a link to the school calendar. Site visitors should not have to dig through the website to find what they need.

- ◆ **Ask—fresh or stale?** Place timely content on the website. Fresh content will motivate people to come back to the site as a trusted source of information For comparison, check out college and university websites for ideas of how to keep the site engaging and dynamic.

- ◆ **Impress the first time!** Teacher candidates form opinions based in large part upon first impressions, and the website will likely be responsible for that impression. In today's increasingly competitive environment, parents want to know that their child will be safe and achieve at high levels. Members of your business community and other members of the "hidden market" want to see that their tax dollars are being used efficiently and effectively. Their first impression may be their only impression.

Use these marketing tools and tactics to help separate your school from other organizations that are competing for similar resources.

12
Making Change Stick

You and the school leadership team have decided to implement a success academy to provide additional support for struggling students. In addition, you are a member of a district-level team considering a revision of the mathematics curriculum scope and sequence for the elementary grades. You are also promoting a shift to using technology more and more in the classroom as a supplement and replacement for the current science textbook and ancillary materials. In each of these situations, you are leading a change effort. Unfortunately, many change efforts stall or fail completely. The term itself, *change effort*, hints at the difficulty many school executives sense about making significant change within their school or district. Yet, there are a number of lessons from successful change leadership initiatives that can give you practical tools and frameworks to lead and manage change effectively.

In this chapter, we will examine three steps that are fundamental to any change effort and consider how they are linked to key issues and implications. In his seminars with senior leaders in the federal government, Jeff Edwards suggests that the three stages of any change leadership can be summarized as Prepare, Implement, and Consolidate (Edwards, 2009). In an earlier chapter, we discussed increasing the use of technology in the classrooms. We'll use that example to illustrate how you might use the three-part framework to drive change within your organization. We'll also tie in research that has been done on change leadership through John Kotter's (2008) work on the eight steps of organizational change.

Prepare

There is a tremendous amount of work that must be done before you can involve others in your change initiative. The key elements in this part of the change initiative are:

- ♦ establish the need for change with a great deal of "urgency" (to use John Kotter's term; Kotter, 2008)

- ♦ bring together your team

♦ determine several solution options

♦ determine a strategy

Gap Analysis

Establishing the need for change comes from an analysis of school data and goals. Jeff Edwards, a professor at the University of North Carolina Kenan-Flagler Business School, suggests that the need for change comes from a gap between where the organization is currently and where it should be. Gaps differ in terms of the content, size, importance, and urgency. A common starting point is to look at your school's achievement levels for student subgroups and compare your school's results with the results of other schools with similar demographics. Your fact pack and the tools that you applied with data driven decision making will come into play at this point. Other data sources may include informal and formal observations, teacher and community satisfaction surveys, reports from district and state education agencies, and data that you gather from informal observations.

For example, let's return to the example on the effectiveness of technology for inquiry-based instruction. To recap: last summer you bought and had installed over 120 computers. You suspect that these computers are not being used to their fullest capacity for inquiry-based instruction. To determine whether there really *is* a gap, you and your assistant principals conducted a quick tally over 2 week's time to determine the number of computers which are being used for instructional purposes. You learned that less than 30% of the computers are being used in any manner. Furthermore, you noticed that some grade levels and teams use the computers more frequently than others, skewing the numbers even more. You've partially established the gap.

You are beginning to know the current state of classroom technology usage and next must determine what the level and type of usage should be. To learn more about what exemplary schools are doing, you call some colleagues and do some online searches to get information. You learn through the Consortium of School Networking (www.cosn.org) that there is compelling evidence that technology helps with inquiry-based education—an instructional focus for you and your school. CoSN gives you additional information and research to bolster your argument (Kleiman, 2009).

Building Your Team

At this point, you and your assistant principals have established the need for change. Yet your teachers and staff, who will be implementing the change, have no idea what you are seeing, what type of problem it is, and why it is a problem. To single-handedly attempt to push this change initiative is folly. In this preparation phase, you must bring together a core team to help you collectively create a sense of urgency to change the status quo. Kotter (2008) suggests that failing to create a sense of urgency is a key element in derailing your change initiative. You have two tasks here in the preparation phase: strategically selecting your team members and creating urgency with the team.

It is tempting to stack your core team with people who frequently agree with you and defer to your judgment. Succumbing to this temptation can serve to derail your change initiative before it starts. Carefully consider the composition of the team and include informal leaders who have the faculty's respect, can influence the discussion, and move your initiative forward. Your core team will be your voice in the many informal conversations that swirl around the change initiative. The core change team should be no more than seven people.

Determining Team Membership

One tactic we have found helpful in determining team membership is to think through the school's informal leaders. These informal leaders may not be on your school leadership team. They just want to teach, but other teachers frequently defer to them and seek their advice.

The following is another way of thinking about your teachers. Place them in four groups called *innovators, first followers, slow movers,* and *laggards.*

- ♦ **Innovators** are those teachers who are already far ahead of you on the topic. This group may be anywhere from 5% to 10% of your faculty.

- ♦ **First followers** are those who may not be the first to embrace the initial wave of the new innovation, but they are willing followers of the first wave. This group of pioneers may be between 10% to 15% of your entire faculty.

- ♦ **Slow movers** are the largest segment in most faculty groups in any type of change initiative. They usually fall between 30% to 50% of your faculty. This "mighty middle" is the group that won't be the ones to take the risk but once they see that it is an accepted way to do things will generally join in the action.

- ♦ **Laggards** are those who will not engage no matter what you say. They will continue to do things the same way they have always done in the past. They think that chalkboards and mimeograph machines are way under-rated and that the best classroom is one where the student desks are bolted to the floor in rows.

As you look at your faculty to determine who might serve on your change team, you find that your trailblazers already have blogs, wikis, and multiple pages in various social networking websites. They instant message at school and have created websites for their students to download notes and homework assignments from their classes along with neat links and WebQuests to encourage further inquiry. Your pioneers may not be the first to embrace the initial wave of the new innovation, but they are willing followers once they see how this new technology works for kids and how it can be used for more than simply electronic drill and practice. Your settlers may be afraid of damaging the computer but do understand how they work and are basically literate in using applications like word processing, spreadsheets, databases, and online searches.

Urgency

John Kotter (2008) differentiates among true urgency, complacency, and false urgency. He suggests that *true urgency* occurs when people come to work *every day* determined to do something to advance the mission of the organization, even if it is for only 15 minutes. *Complacency* occurs when people think that what they are doing is just fine, but that other people have to make changes to move the organization forward. *False urgency* is frenetic behavior, such as endless meetings, presentations, and another series of numbing taskforce meetings with nothing to show for all the time involved.

After analyzing the data, the urgency for change is clear. You may be disappointed if you simply present the data to your team and expect them to reach the same conclusion. They will not be inspired by a PowerPoint presentation with charts, tables, and graphs. Chip and Dan Heath (2007) call this the "curse of knowledge." You need to create a sense of urgency using some real, concrete, and tangible examples to illustrate the issues. This approach will help rally the team and lead them to understand the urgency of the situation. You may decide to take your team on a field trip to observe how a similar school is using technology for inquiry-based instruction. Or, you may decide to get a stack of play money and use it to illustrate a comparison of what you have spent with the money that is not being used.

Developing a Strategy

Once you have the team's attention and they understand the urgency of the situation, you can guide them to look at different options to reduce the gap. You can use the same discipline and model that you used in your strategy development:

♦ Determine what you want to accomplish and the assumptions behind it.

♦ Lead discussion with the core team to look at multiple ways to accomplish the goal.

♦ Evaluate which of those options or combinations of options have the greatest chance of success. Outline what needs to be done, by whom, and by when.

Your strategy is what will be laid out to the entire faculty. If you possibly can, let team members take the lead in presenting the strategy and vision to your entire faculty, as it is they who have determined what to do and can help create that sense of urgency with the faculty. With your support, they should take ownership of telling the story and building a case for change.

The key tasks in the preparation phase are to determine the gap, get the right people on the team, and find concrete ways to make the issue real and concrete to the core team. You haven't rolled out any new initiative to your entire faculty yet. This preparation stage is essential to giving your change initiative the best chance for success. Invest your time with your informal leaders and get their ideas, rather than outlining what critical tasks need to be accomplished. *Do not skip this important step.* Without investing the time building support from informal networks among the staff, your change initiative may be doomed to failure.

Implement

To start the implementation phase, look for ways to communicate the team's vision and how to get there. Use the same types of stories that worked in creating the urgency message and need for change. Don't let your ego get in the way of who tells the stories. Focus on the end result. The more you can get the team to take ownership and tell the story to the larger group, the greater the effectiveness.

Telling the Story to a Larger Group

Your team may determine they need to have professional development in using the web as an instructional tool to increase the use of technology for inquiry-based learning. You can set the stage to communicate the story by sending everybody a short summary of the issue on which the team has been working. You might follow it up with a short pre-reading to help provide background on the issue. The first meeting should be led by team members who will set the stage by sharing the story that illustrates the urgency of the issue. They outline the issue, why it is important, and share what they see as the strategy going forward. They emphasize that it is a draft strategy and that they welcome other ideas that will help move the resolution of the challenge more quickly.

Publicly thank the team members for their hard work and effort. Invite teachers to comment on the strategy, and encourage them to share their ideas. At the conclusion of each meeting, have someone record and summarize suggestions and establish a deadline for input. Notice that we did not mention whether or not people agreed with the strategy. It is human nature to maintain the status quo. You are giving people the opportunity to improve on the plan, but not offering them a way out of the plan.

Remove Roadblocks for Your Team and Their Allies

The team has decided upon a multiprong approach:

- ♦ Provide substitute days for small groups of teachers who will go and see how other teachers use technology and agree to come back to teach others what they learned.

- ♦ Provide a series of short in-service sessions by some of the trailblazers who are currently using technology in their classrooms.

- ♦ Substitute release time for people to volunteer to write at least one web-related instructional activity per unit for each grade level.

During the planning session, you pushed hard for performance metrics that focus upon the use of technology in the classroom. Simply using the number of web-based instructional activities written and distributed will not assess the impact on student learn. You also have, as a result of the small team meeting, reallocated some money to support this initiative.

The next step is to turn the team loose to act on the plan. Identify roadblocks that will impede their ability to implement the plan. Fortunately, trailblazers will generally get with other trailblazers to implement the strategies. Pioneers will talk with other pioneers, and the settlers will ask questions, trying to find out how the new idea is working.

Do not look for wholesale change from the entire group. There will be a very small group of people who are going to try this new way of teaching. Your role as a leader is to encourage their efforts by demonstrating interest and checking in to see what they are doing. Look for opportunities to remove roadblocks to make it easier for them to continue down the path. It will also be important to get updates on what they are trying, what they are learning, and how they are making progress against the performance metrics that were laid out in the initial planning. You are essentially running a small "research and development" lab where you are trying to see what is working and what is not working. Be sure to give credit and encouragement when the pioneers are taking risk and learning from failure. That is part of your role as well. You are empowering others to act, test, and revise.

In this example, your technology trailblazers have already contacted their network around the country through discussion boards and websites that offer web-enabled content to support the inquiry-based learning approach. They share what they have learned, what has worked, and what has not worked well. They share their information with the informal team and invite others to visit their classrooms. Some teachers on your team are reluctant to have people come into their classroom, but share their lesson and unit plans in faculty and grade/department level meetings. You are looking for some small and early wins. The "big win" occurs when you find some trailblazers or pioneers experimenting with technology and then see gains in student achievement. You are endorsing and giving encouragement to the trailblazers and pioneers, while drawing increased attention to the work and success of the strategy to the settlers. Settlers are generally waiting to find out "if this is for real" or if the change initiative is simply a passing fad. Your continued encouragement and public acclamation helps to keep classroom technology usage in the public eye. Seize any opportunity to publicly and privately encourage people using technology that also supports inquiry-based instruction.

Your role here is to be almost like a cheerleader. Formally and informally encourage and publicize the successes and challenges of technology usage. You also use the formal organization to provide resources and track what is being done against the performance metrics established by the committee. Faculty and PTA meetings are also excellent venues to recognize the efforts of your staff.

In the case of our example of using technology to facilitate inquiry-based instruction, you may have only 5 to 10 (including the core team) who would be considered trailblazers and pioneers on a faculty of 50. One principal noted that her actions were like building a big snowball—starting with a small handful of snow, molding and compacting, then adding more and more snow. Pretty soon, she said, you have a pretty big snow ball that you can simply roll more and more snow around and watch it get bigger and bigger.

Finding Pockets of Resistance

You will not reach all people at the same time. One principal said that in his experience, "the only person I know that likes change is a baby with a wet diaper." It is unrealistic to think that you will get 100% buy-in from your entire faculty. People may tell you that they are for the change, but they are unwilling to change their actions and behaviors. In fact, the more you push them, the harder they will dig in their heels.

One common yet ineffective practice for school leaders is to spend their time cajoling, pushing, or forcing those who are unwilling to change. This yields little in terms of positive result. Recognize that you are not going to get everybody on board at the same time. In the beginning, you will be able to bring along about 25% of your team.

Instead, spend your time, effort, and energy on those who are working to implement the strategy: your innovators, first followers, and slow movers who have started on the change initiative. Spend time in their classrooms, ask them what they are doing, what is and is not working, and what lessons they have learned. Publicize them in as many different forums as you can, such as faculty meetings, PTA meetings, informal meetings with community members, in newsletters, blogs (a key forum, especially if you are trying to communicate the benefit of using technology), and any other manner that can encourage them to continue their work. You want to nurture and grow their success and have them demonstrate that success. Proven success (proof of concept) is a currency that will help many of your slow movers and first followers to try the new behaviors. They are watching to see how you respond and interact with various groups. You know you have another ally when you have a person come up to you and ask for more information. Walk them to one of your success stories and let them talk—you need to stay in the background and let your successful innovators or first followers tell their story.

Consolidate

You've worked with your core team to build a good set of lessons to share with the larger group. Ideally, you've found that the actual gains have exceeded the targets laid out initially in your performance metrics. You and your team have also tweaked some areas and completely discarded other areas that simply didn't work. You're now ready to consolidate these gains, share them with the entire group, and start executing your strategy on a larger scale. You have data to support that using technology for inquiry-based learning helps with student achievement. You have a small but growing group of teachers who are successfully using technology and seeing the results. It's easy at this point to try to create a data-filled PowerPoint presentation with charts and graphs and cool pictures to publicize your success. Yet, we'll suggest that you will be more effective by having your first group of teachers tell their story and share what they have learned first. Start with your first followers , then have the innovators flesh out the details. The innovators can then serve as the expert consultants along with the first followers . You want to allow your core team to evangelize and get the glory and public acclaim.

Up to this point, you have been focusing your efforts more informally and with a small group of people. You now want to expand the practice to a more formal and organizational level. In the consolidation phase, you serve more as a consultant who asks some pretty hard questions during grade level or department meetings. You sit in on these meetings to simultaneously serve as a host or maitre d' to link up people and to offer to help teachers find ways to leverage the lessons learned from your first group of teachers.

You will still encounter pockets of resistance in this phase. You are not trying to get 100% of your faculty on board. In fact, if you can get 60% on board, you will have created a critical mass in which you can claim success. For those pockets of resistance, your friendly and candid questioning about comparing the gap between "the old way" and what you are seeing with those who are consistently implementing the strategy is a powerful tool to start the discussion.

It will be wise, when talking to people residing in the pockets of resistance, to focus on student success. Do their students have the ability to apply concepts to more advanced analysis on the end-of-unit assessments that are jointly created and administered? Their response can provide a springboard to a discussion about what they are doing and how effective it is and to contrasting that against what you are seeing in other classrooms. You're asking questions like, "How is what you are doing more effective than what I am seeing in classrooms where the teacher is incorporating technology?" You want to offer to help in any way that you can. Make it clear in these conversations that you are interested in supporting them while at the same time expecting and requiring high levels of achievement. Always invite them to find a better way, but until they find that better way, you expect them to do what is in the best interest of the students, not in the interest of their individual comfort level.

Continue to look at setting the stage for building the capacity for change. You know that this single change initiative will not be the last one for your school. You want to build the capacity for people to innovate, experiment, and cycle through the steps in change leadership with greater agility and velocity. Next time you are hoping for a "change initiative" rather than a "change effort."

References

Allen, D. (2002). *Getting things done: The art of stress-free productivity*. New York: Penguin.

Bazerman, M., & Moore, D. (2008). *Managerial decision making*. Hoboken, NJ: Wiley.

Bradt, G., Check, J., & Pedraza, J. (2009). *The new leader's 100-Day Action Plan*. Hoboken, NJ: Wiley.

Cable, D. (2007). *Change to strange*. Upper Saddle River, NJ: Wharton Business School Publishing.

Chester, E. (2002). *Employing generation why?* Lakewood, CO: Tucker House Books.

Ciampa, D., & Watkins, M. (2008, January/February). Rx for New CEOs. *Chief Executive*, 29–32.

Coble, L. (2005). *Lessons learned from experience*. Greensboro, NC: On Track Press.

Collins, J. (2005). *Good to great and the social sectors*. New York: Harper Collins.

Coyne, K., Coyne, P., & Coyne, S. (2008, April/May). New CEO, Old Team, *Chief Executive*, 54–58.

Daly, P., & Watkins, M. (with Reavis, C.). (2006). *The first 90 Days in government*. Boston: Harvard Business School Press.

Deal, T., & Peterson, K. (2009). *Shaping school culture*. San Francisco: Jossey-Bass.

Dotlich, D., & Cairo, P. (2003). *Why CEOs fail*. San Francisco: Jossey-Bass.

Drucker, P. (2006). *Managing the nonprofit organization*. New York: HarperCollins Paperback.

Eblin, S. (2008). *The next level*. Mountain View, CA: Davies-Black Publishing.

Edwards, J. (2009). *Three phases of change*. Unpublished paper.

Fogg, P. (2008). When generations collide. *The Chronicle of Higher Education, 54*(45), 18–23.

Goldsmith, M. (2007). *What got you here won't get you there*. New York: Hyperion.

Gronbach, K. (2008). *The age curve*. New York: AMACON.

Grove, A. (1999). *Only the paranoid survive*. New York: Broadway Business.

Hammond, J., Keeney, R., & Raiffa, H. (2002). *Smart choices*. New York: Broadway Publishing.

Harris, T. (2004). *I'm OK, You're OK*. New York: Harper Collins.

Heath, C., & Heath, D. (2007). *Made to stick*. New York: Random House.

Hersey, P., & Blanchard, K. (2009). *Management of organizational behavior* (9th ed.). Upper Saddle River, NJ: Prentice Hall.

Howe, N., & Strauss, W. (2008). *Millennials and K-12 Schools*. Great Falls, VA: LifeCourse Associates.

Hyatt, M. (March 4, 2007). *The importance of the weekly review*. Retrieved July 20, 2009, from http://michaelhyatt.com/2007/03/the-importance-of-the-weekly-review.html

Johnson, S. (2004). *Finders and keepers*. San Francisco: Jossey-Bass.

Kleiman, G. (2009). *Does Technology Enhance Inquiry-Based Learning?* Consortium of School Networking. Retrieved March 10, 2009, from Consortium of School Networking Web site:http://www.cosn.org/Resources/ResourceLibrary/tabid/4189/id/28/Default.aspx

Kotler, P. (2006). *Marketing management* (12th ed.). New York: Prentice Hall.

Kotter, J. (2008). *A Sense of Urgency*. Boston: Harvard Business School Press.

Kroll, L., Miller, M., & Sarafin, T. (Eds.). (2009, March 11). *The world's billionaires*. [Special Report]. Retrieved August 31, 2009, from http://www.forbes.com

Kyler, J. (2003). *Assessing your external environment: STEEP analysis*. Retrieved June 25, 2009, from http://www.comptia.com

Lancaster, L., & Stillman, D. (2005). If I pass the baton, who will grab it? *Public Management, 87*(8), 8–15.

Lancaster, L., & Stillman, D. (2006, June). Here come the millennials. *Twin Cities Business*, 63–68.

Lawler, E. (2008). *Talent: Making people your competitive advantage*. San Francisco: Jossey-Bass

Lencioni, P. (2004). *Death by meeting*. San Francisco: Jossey-Bass

Lombardo, M., & Eichinger, R. (1989). *Preventing derailment*. Greensboro, NC: Center for Creative Leadership.

Lovallo, D., & Kahneman, D. (2003, July). Delusions of success. *Harvard Business Review, (81)*7. Retrieved November 15, 2008, from http://hbr.harvardbusiness.org/

Ludeman, K., & Erlandson, E. (2006). *Alpha male syndrome*. Boston: Harvard Business School Press.

MacCormack, A. (2004, May). *Management lessons from Mars*, Harvard Business Review, *82*(5). Retrieved December 12, 2008, from http://hbr.harvardbusiness.org/

Maister, D. (2003), *Managing the professional services firm*. New York: Free Press.

Martin, C., & Tulgan, B. (2001). *Managing Generation Y*. Amherst, MA: HRD Press.

Martin, C., & Tulgan, B. (2006). *Managing the generation mix.* Amherst, MA: HRD Press.

McKenna, P., & Maister, D. (2005). *First among equals: How to manage a group of professionals.* New York: Free Press.

National Comprehensive Center for Teacher Quality and Public Agenda. (2008). *Lessons learned: New teachers talk about their jobs, challenges, and long-range plans.* New York: Public Agenda Foundation.

National Education Association. (2003). *Status of the American Public School Teacher 2000-2001.* Washington, DC: Author.

Nielson, J. (2005) *Top ten web design mistakes of 2005.* Retrieved June 25, 2009, from http://www.useit.com/alertbox/designmistakes.html

Oncken, W. (1987), *Managing management time.* New York: Prentice Hall.

Page, S. (2008). *The difference: How the power of diversity creates better groups, firms, schools, and societies.* Princeton, MA: Princeton University Press.

Peters, T. (1996). *Liberation management.* New York: Ballantine Books.

Peters, T. (1999a) *The brand you 50.* New York: Knopf.

Peters, T. (1999b) *The professional service firm 50.* New York: Knopf.

Peterson, K. (2001, Winter). The roar of complexity. *Journal of Staff Development, 22*(1), 18–21 .

Pfeffer, J., & Sutton, R. (2000). *The knowing-doing gap.* Boston: Harvard Business School Press.

Raisel, E., & Friga, P. (2001). *The McKinsey mind.* New York: McGraw Hill.

Robbins, S. (2004, January 19). *How Leaders Use Questions.* Retrieved February 3, 2009, from http://www.steverrobbins.com/articles/HBSWK/howleadersusequestions.htm

Robert Half International & Yahoo! (2008). *What millennial workers want.* Retrieved August 31, 2009, from http://www.hotjobsresources.com/pdfs/MillennialWorkers.pdf

Rubinstein, J., Meyer, D., & Evans, J. (2001). Executive control of cognitive processes in task switching. *Journal of Experimental Psychology—Human Perception and Performance, 27*(4), 763–797.

Simon, H. (1997). *Administrative behavior* (4th ed.). New York: Free Press.

Smart, B. (1999). *Topgrading.* New York: Prentice Hall.

Stuart, A. (2005), Motivating the Middle, *CFO.* Retrieved July 1, 2009, from http://www.cfo.com/article.cfm/4443660/c_4448927?f=insidecfo)

Sull, D. (2007). Closing the gap between strategy and execution. *MIT Sloan Management Review, 48*(4), 31–38.

Thull, J. (2005). *The Prime Solution,* New York: Kaplan Busines.

Townsend, R. (1995). *The B-2 chronicles: Uncommon wisdom for un-corporate America.* New York: Perigree Trade.

Livingston, A. (2007). *Conditions of Education, 2007 in brief* (IES Publication No. NCES 2007006). Washington, DC: U.S. Department of Education, Institute of Educational Sciences, National Center for Education Statistics.

Vermi, N., Greenslade, S., & Armatys, M. A. (2008, May). Taking the Talent Pulse: What Drives High Potentials, *Talent Management*, 34–37.

Winston, S. (2004). *Organized for Success*. New York: Crown.